RENTING and LETTING

a Consumer Publication

Consumers' Association
publishers of **Which?**
14 Buckingham Street
London WC2N 6DS

a Consumer Publication

edited by Edith Rudinger

published by Consumers' Association
publishers of **Which?**

Consumer publications
are available from
Consumers' Association
and from booksellers.
Details are given at
the end of this book.

© Consumers' Association March 1985

ISBN 0 340 35249 3
     0 85202 276 X

photoset by Paston Press, Norwich
printed in Great Britain

contents

This book describes the legal implications
of renting or letting a home
in the private or public sector
in England and Wales.
It does not apply in Scotland
and Northern Ireland.

introduction

The law relating to landlord and tenant is complicated. Over the past sixty years, successive governments have added layers of new laws, rules and regulations in an attempt to protect tenants, and control landlords' income from land, and promote the supply of housing.

At the beginning of the twentieth century, the majority of lettings were by private landlords for investment purposes. By and large, tenants were free to remain in their rented homes undisturbed for as long as they liked, with little or no alteration in the rent. After the first world war, the demand for housing was greater than the supply, and rents soared. A landlord could easily rid himself of a tenant who could not afford to pay a higher rent, by serving a simple notice to quit, and then letting to a new tenant at that higher rent. Parliament introduced the Increase of Rent and Mortgage Interest (War Restrictions) Act 1915, preventing landlords who owned homes within specified rateable values from increasing the rent, and limiting their right to recover possession. Although the 1915 Act was intended to be a temporary measure, provisions to control rents and give tenants security of tenure have regulated lettings in the private sector ever since (apart from a short period of decontrol in the 1950's). It was not until 1980 that this security was extended to council tenants.

Today, the principal Acts governing the private sector include:

○ the *Rent Act 1977* as amended by the *Housing Act 1980* under which most lettings by private landlords fall;

○ the *Housing Act 1961* imposing compulsory repair obligations on landlords of short lettings (that is, seven years or less);

○ the *Landlord and Tenant Act 1954* encompassing long leases at low rents, leases of premises with mixed residential and business use and lettings by an approved private body;

○ the *Leasehold Reform Act 1967* which gives tenants of houses held under a long lease at a low rent the right to call for an extended lease or the freehold;

○ The *Housing Act 1980*, as amended by the *Housing and Building Control Act 1984*, which regulates the rights of council tenants;

○ The *Protection from Eviction Act 1977* affords a basic protection against unlawful eviction and harassment to all 'residential occupiers', in both the private and public sector.

leases and licences

English law recognises two forms of legal ownership of land only, freehold and leasehold. A lease is basically a contract which establishes the relationship of landlord and tenant. The landlord grants the tenant the exclusive right to enjoy his land (which includes the buildings on it) for a set time in consideration for the regular payment of a sum of money, the rent.

The contract defines the rights and liabilities of the parties, in what are sometimes called 'covenants'. Common examples are covenants to repair, covenants restricting the use of the property and covenants against the tenant parting with possession (such as sub-letting or mortgaging). When the contract expires, the land reverts to the landlord, except where the law provides otherwise. His interest during the lifetime of the lease is called 'the reversion'. A validly created lease remains binding on any subsequent purchaser of the reversion (that is, a new landlord).

The landlord need not necessarily be the freeholder. He may have only a leasehold interest himself, but can create out of his own lease a sub-lease to another person. There may be many such interests in one property. The freeholder is the head-landlord. The parties between him and the actual occupier will be both tenants under the lease they hold and landlords under the lease they grant. They are sometimes called 'intermediate' or 'mesne' landlords. Each underlease must be for a period that is at least one day shorter than the lease out of which it has been created.

A lease is not the same as a contract for the hire of goods, such as a car for instance. A person who hires a car can drive it where and when he pleases, but he gets no rights of ownership over the car. A lease confers on the tenant an interest in the land. He can sell ('assign') this interest, mortgage it, leave it by will, grant a sub-lease and so on.

Granting a lease is not the only way in which a freeholder can profit from letting someone live in his vacant property. He can merely permit someone to stay there, so that his being on the property is not a trespass. It can be agreed that the permission should last for a certain length of time and a sum similar to rent may be charged for the occupation. Such an arrangement is known as a licence. A guest staying at a hotel is a licensee, and so are lodgers and theatregoers.

licence

A licence is a personal arrangement between the licensor and the licensee. It usually forms part of a contract and can therefore be terminated in accordance with the terms of the contract. A licensee has no proprietary interest and his licence does not bind a third party: if a new landlord buys the premises, he has the right to evict the licensee who lives there, even if he knew of the arrangement at the time of buying. All that the licensee can do is to sue the previous licensor for breach of contract. But the courts have, on rare occasions, decided that a particular licence was irrevocable and capable of binding a third party purchaser, where to do otherwise would have caused gross injustice.

The main reason for distinguishing between a lease and a licence is that most of the statutory provisions which confer considerable protection on tenants do not apply to licensees. A licence may therefore be offered by land owners who wish to enjoy an income from their property without being bound by controlled rents and sitting tenants. The courts have said on several occasions that it is neither illegal nor contrary to public policy to use the licence to avoid the Rent Acts, although they should be on the look-out for leases dressed up as licences.

In a case of dispute, a person who occupies as his home property belonging to another will obviously be keen to establish that he has a lease rather than a licence. A landlord may wish to establish the opposite.

It is, therefore, in the interests of those letting and renting accommodation to look more closely at the lease/licence distinction.

characteristics of a lease, and how a licence differs from it

A lease, apart from conferring a legal interest in the property, confers, in essence, the right to exclusive possession for a definite period.

The length of the lease must be certain. A definite period can mean:

(i) a single period ending on a specified date, for example after 99 years. This is a fixed term lease.

In a fixed term lease, the maximum duration must be known. It does not matter that the lease contains provisions which mean that it may be ended prematurely. For example, at the beginning of the second world war it became common to grant leases 'for the duration of the war', but it was established that such a grant was void because no one knew when the war would end. Temporary legislation was introduced to convert these grants into ten-year leases (so that the maximum duration was known) terminable by one month's notice by either party at the end of the war. This device can be used in any case where it is desired that a lease should end on the happening of an uncertain event. For example, if a tenant is waiting for his newly-built house to be finished, he will give a month's notice to end the fixed term lease of his present accommodation when his new house is ready.

In fact, most fixed term leases contain provisions for premature determination. It would be rare to find a fixed term lease which does not allow the landlord to bring the lease to an end if, for example, the tenant does not pay the rent.

(ii) a short but definite period in the first place (a month, a week, a year) which will continue for further periods of that length until ended by notice to quit. This is known as a periodic tenancy.

In a periodic tenancy, the minimum duration is always known: a month, a year, a week or whatever period the tenancy was initially granted for. The maximum duration of a periodic tenancy can never be known until one party serves a notice to quit.

is it a lease or a licence?

Having a lease, i.e. being a leaseholder, is synonymous with being a tenant.

If the occupier does not have exclusive possession there cannot be a lease. Exclusive possession means that the tenant has the right to exclude everybody else from the premises, including the landlord. If the landlord retains control of the premises, as is usual in the case of a hotel, for example, there can only be a licence.

At one time, exclusive possession was the decisive factor in determining whether a lease or a licence had been created. If the occupier had exclusive possession he was a tenant; if he did not, he was a lodger, a mere licensee. However, the tests the courts apply have become more sophisticated so that now it is almost impossible to predict a court's decision in any particular case. Whether it is a lease or a licence now depends on the intention of the parties, to be inferred from the surrounding circumstances. In the words of Lord Denning, when he was Master of the Rolls: "*What is the test to see whether the occupier of [accommodation] is a tenant or a licensee? It does not depend on whether he or she has exclusive possession or not. It does not depend on whether the [accommodation] is furnished or not. It does not depend on whether the occupation is permanent or temporary. It does not depend on the label which parties put upon it. All these are factors which may influence the decision but none of them is conclusive. All the circumstances have to be worked out. Eventually, the answer depends on the nature and quality of the occupancy. Was it intended that the occupier should have a stake in the [accommodation] or did he have only permission for himself personally to occupy the [accommodation], whether under a contract or not? In which case he is a licensee.*"

Here are some of the factors which, in decided cases, have swayed the courts either in favour of a lease or in favour of a licence.

six factors which may indicate a lease:

(i) *exclusive possession:*   If an agreement precludes exclusive possession there can be no tenancy. The fact that the landlord has the right to come in to inspect the premises and carry out repairs on giving notice to the tenant, does not detract from the occupier's exclusive possession. On the contrary, it reinforces it: in a true tenancy, the landlord commits trespass if he enters the premises without the consent of the tenant. Where there is a licence, the landlord has the right to enter the property without notice or consent.

(ii) *an intention to grant the tenant a stake in the premises:*   This intention to create the relationship of landlord and tenant can usually be gleaned from the agreement itself, such as referring to the parties as 'the landlord' and 'the tenant'. Other examples are:

○ giving the landlord a restricted right to enter the premises (as in (i) above);

○ prohibiting sub-letting (a licensee has nothing to sub-let);

○ providing that the landlord can end the tenancy if the tenant breaks any of his covenants.

(iii) *other terms of the agreement:*   Terms which point towards the occupier having rights in the premises, that is being a tenant, are:

○ obligation to repair

○ the right to quiet possession.

(iv) *a fixed term:*   This is more likely to be a lease than a licence.

(v) *the payment of rent:*   Rent is technically money paid for the use and occupation of premises, but can include money paid for services connected with that occupation, for example electricity, gas and water. The use of the word 'rent', the provision of a rent book or rent receipts is strong evidence of a tenancy. Tenants should be sure to keep records of payment of rent (cheque-stubs, receipts, bank statements and so on) as otherwise it can sometimes be difficult to prove that rent was paid.

(vi) *payment of rates by the occupier.*

seven factors which may indicate a licence:

(i) *denial of exclusive possession:* If the agreement does not give the occupier exclusive possession, he is a mere licensee. 'Non-exclusive licenses' which private landlords use normally give the landlord, and/or a third party chosen by him, the right to share the accommodation with the licensee. But if it can be shown that the landlord had no intention of ever enforcing this right, it being a mere device to disguise the true nature of the transaction, it will not prevent a tenancy from arising.

(ii) *an intention to grant a personal right to occupy premises rather than a stake in them:* This would create the relationship of licensor and licensee only. Describing the parties as 'the licensor' and 'the licensee' shows such an intention, and so does giving the licensee 'the right to occupy', rather than 'the use and enjoyment' of the premises. A declaration signed by the licensee stating that he knew that he was entering a licence as opposed to a tenancy agreement, is strong evidence that the parties intended to create a licence. There may be a provision in the contract that the parties are willing to enter into the agreement on this basis only.

(iii) *expressing the agreement to be of a personal nature:* and therefore not capable of any assignment.

(iv) *a very short-term agreement for accommodation.*

(v) *specific terms (or lack of them) in the agreement:* The following are all indicative of a licence:

   o provision for the payment of a 'licence fee'

   o making the licensee responsible for 'breakages and damage'

   o giving the landlord the right to terminate the agreement within a short time for non-payment of the licence fee

   o the licensee not being made responsible for repairs or for the payment of rates

   o the landlord reserving to himself a right of entry in order to inspect and repair.

(vi) ***language used:*** A licence is usually in much more informal language than a lease.

(vii) ***services:*** The landlord retaining overall control of the premises and/or providing meals or cleaning services, or both (for example residents in an old folks' home and youths in a hostel are licensees).

A 'licensee' who suspects he is a tenant should seek legal advice; the matter may have to be resolved by a county court judge.

Two 1978 cases, decided by the courts within weeks of each other, show how fine a line can sometimes exist between a lease and a licence. Both cases concerned almost identical non-exclusive licence agreements for bed-sitting rooms. In the first case, the potential occupiers were told that the clause giving the landlady or a person of her choice the right to share the bed-sit was a mere formality and would never be exercised. This, together with the fact that the occupiers were looking for accommodation 'to rent', led the court to decide that they had a tenancy. In the second case, however, it was proved that the occupier knew he was entering a licence agreement and was so desperate for accommodation that he would have accepted anything. He had a licence.

Furthermore, a recent case has shown that it is possible for a landlord to grant exclusive possession without creating a tenancy, provided that the rest of the agreement is consistent with a licence.

creating a lease

A lease for a term of three years or less may be created orally (by word of mouth) or in writing. This includes a periodic tenancy, even though it may in fact continue for much longer than three years by being automatically renewed. For a lease for over three years to be effective at law, it must be created by deed. A deed is a formal written document which must be 'signed, sealed and delivered'. It only becomes operative when all these three requirements have been satisfied.

A lease for over three years that has not been created by deed may nonetheless be valid as 'an agreement for a lease', sometimes called an equitable lease. So, if there is a document that fails to create a legal lease because it is not a deed, but it is in writing, the court will treat the written grant (the 'equitable lease') as a legal lease provided it is just in all the circumstances to do so. Similarly, if the parties have made a written agreement for the grant of a legal lease but no deed was ever executed, the court will treat the agreement as if it were a legal lease and the parties will be in the same position as if it had been properly created.

Even if there is only an oral grant or agreement, the court will treat it as a grant of a legal lease if the tenant has partly performed the agreement. He will have done so if he has entered into possession of the premises and started paying rent. But, of course, this will only work if there is sufficient proof of an oral agreement to grant a lease in the first place.

registration of equitable lease
The courts are willing to enforce an equitable lease but it needs to be protected, otherwise a person who later buys the landlord's

interest (the reversion) will 'take free' from the equitable lease – that is, he will not be bound by that lease. This protection is achieved by registration by the tenant.

An equitable lease of unregistered land must be registered as a land charge; if of registered land, a notice or caution has to be entered against the landlord's title. The Land Charges Department at Plymouth (telephone Plymouth 779831) will tell you how to register a land charge; the Central Land Registry in London (telephone 01-405 3488) how to lodge a notice or caution.

In the case of registered land, registering an equitable lease is less vital, because an 'equitable' tenant who is in occupation of premises at the time of a later sale will have what is known as an 'overriding interest' and a purchaser who has not enquired of him whether he has any rights in those premises will not be bound by that overriding interest.

getting only a periodic tenancy

Even where there is neither a properly created legal nor an equitable lease, the tenant still gets something. The law presumes that a tenant who goes into possession of property and pays rent periodically has a periodic tenancy, measured by when he pays the rent. Thus, if he pays rent monthly he has a monthly tenancy; weekly, a weekly tenancy; yearly, a yearly tenancy. And because it is for under three years, it can be legal even though created orally. Such a tenancy will most probably be protected by the Rent Act, so that even though the tenant has not got quite what he bargained for, he is well protected. If the tenancy falls outside the Rent Act, however, the tenant is in a much more vulnerable position: an unprotected periodic tenancy can be ended by one month's notice if rent is paid weekly or monthly; by six months' notice if rent is paid yearly.

It is better for a lease for even under three years to be in writing, rather than created orally, to avoid later arguments. Furthermore, where there are no express terms, the law implies certain terms into a lease, which may not be satisfactory to either party.

a licence only

A lease cannot be granted by someone who has no power to do so. If a private landlord forms a company and states in its rules that the company has no power to create a tenancy, then any letting arrangement that the company makes must be a licence and nothing else.

For a private landlord contemplating granting a licence for residential accommodation, there are standard licence agreements available. However, because of the obvious confusion surrounding the lease/licence distinction, he may be better advised to ask a solicitor to draw up the licence agreement. For a relatively simple agreement, the cost would be about £150 in London, slightly less elsewhere.

repair and maintenance

The following comments relate to leases only. A licensor-landlord has to repair and maintain the premises himself; if a so-called 'licence' imposes an obligation on the licensee to repair, the likelihood is that the arrangement is in reality a lease.

covenants to repair

A lease may contain express provision (that is, a covenant) about the repairing obligations of either party or both parties. A tenant who covenants 'to repair' does not have to remedy defects which are already in the premises when the lease is granted. One who covenants 'to keep in repair' or 'to put and keep in repair' has to do any repairs that are necessary at the beginning of the lease. The word 'repair' does not include improving the property but may involve renewals or replacements.

In the last resort, the court will decide whether or not work that needs doing falls within a tenant's covenant, by reference to the covenant. Where a covenant excepts 'fair wear and tear', the tenant is not responsible for dilapidations arising from natural causes, such as age or weathering. If the premises are damaged by fire, the established rule is that if the tenant is responsible for repairs, he must go on paying the rent and re-build the premises (unless the lease states otherwise).

If the tenant covenants to repair, the landlord usually reserves the right to enter the premises and view the state of repair.

If the landlord covenants to repair, he has an implied right to enter the premises to view the state of repair and to effect repairs. But unless he actually knows about the defect, he is liable to repair only if the tenant gives him notice of the disrepair.

no covenants to repair

If there is no express provision in the lease, the law implies a duty on the part of the tenant to repair, but the extent of this depends on the length of his lease. A weekly or monthly tenant has no duty to repair as such, but must not deliberately change the character of the premises (so he cannot make any alterations) and must use them in a 'tenant-like' manner, that is take proper care of them – as Lord Denning said "*by doing those little jobs like unblocking sinks, sweeping chimneys, mending fuses which a reasonable tenant would do (or get his wife to do)*". A yearly tenant must do such repairs as are necessary for him to be able to give up the premises at the end of the term in the same condition as he acquired them.

At common law, there is no implied obligation on the landlord either to put the premises into a state of repair at the beginning of the term of the lease, or to do repairs during the term. A landlord who owns and lets flats in a high-rise block may be under a duty to maintain essential communal facilities, such as lifts. The landlord who lets furnished residential accommodation gives an implied warranty that the accommodation is fit for human habitation.

repairs under the Housing Act 1961

Landlords, especially local authorities, rarely covenant to repair in residential leases; statute has therefore intervened – but only with regard to short-term tenancies. The Housing Act 1961 applies to any tenancy granted after 24 October 1961 which, when granted, was for less than seven years, including periodic tenancies. It imposes on the landlord the duty to repair the structure and exterior of the building. This covers anything that can be regarded as an essential integral part of the structure or exterior of the flat. Thus, repair of the roof would come within the landlord's Housing Act liability towards the tenant of a top floor flat.

Under the Act, the landlord is given responsibility for keeping in repair and proper working order any basins, sinks, baths and other sanitary installations, and any installations for supplying water, gas and electricity for heating. There has been some litigation concerning the extent of the landlord's obligations under the Act in respect of any one individual flat in a block he owns. It seems that he is only responsible for repairing installations within the flat and not in respect of the whole block. A tenant with faulty central heating would therefore have problems if the fault was located in the main central heating boiler in the basement. Repair of the boiler might, however, come within the landlord's implied obligation at common law to keep communal facilities in working order.

If the landlord is responsible for repairs under the Act, he or an agent authorised by him in writing may, at reasonable times of the day and provided he gives the tenant 24 hours notice in writing, enter the property to inspect the state of repair.

The parties cannot contract out of the Act without the permission of the county court.

other laws affecting landlord's duty

There are other statutory provisions which affect a landlord's liability to repair. The Occupier's Liability Act provides that where the landlord retains part of a building under his control (common entrances, for instance), he owes a duty of care to the tenant and his visitors. The Defective Premises Act states that if the landlord has an obligation or right to repair, he owes a duty to anyone who might reasonably be affected by the lack of repair.

tenant not meeting his repairing obligations

If the tenant breaks his covenant (express or implied) to repair, the landlord has two choices: forfeit the lease or sue for damages.

landlord trying to enforce tenant's covenant

Provided the lease contains a covenant to repair and a provision that the landlord can repossess the property if the covenant is broken, the landlord may forfeit the tenant's lease – that is, bring it to an end. The landlord must first serve a notice on the tenant (under section 146 of the Law of Property Act 1925) which

(i) specifies the breach (usually done by preparing a schedule of dilapidations);

(ii) requires it to be remedied;

(iii) asks for compensation, if this is desired.

The tenant must be allowed a reasonable time to comply with the notice. If he does not comply, the landlord can proceed with the forfeiture, by bringing a possession action in the High Court or, more usually, serving a county court notice of intention to seek possession. Proceedings for recovery of possession have to be taken in the county court if the rateable value of the premises at the time of the proceedings brings them within the county court's jurisdiction (most residential lettings will fall within its jurisdiction): the value limit is at present £5,000.

The tenant has the right to apply to the court not to have his lease forfeited. He must make his application before the landlord regains possession of the premises. This relief will be granted if it is just and fair in all the circumstances and subject to such conditions as the court thinks fit. In the case of a repairing covenant, the tenant will probably be told to do the repairs within a certain period.

A sub-tenant is also affected: if the tenant's lease is ended, his lease goes too. If the tenant does not ask for, or is not granted relief from forfeiting his lease, but a sub-tenant is, the sub-tenant is then put in a direct relationship with the landlord for the rest of the term of his sub-tenancy.

The other choice the landlord has if the tenant breaks his covenant to repair, is to sue the tenant for damages for breach of covenant. But a landlord cannot get a court order to force the tenant to carry out repairs.

tenant trying to enforce landlord's covenant to repair

If the landlord (private individual or a local authority) breaks his covenant to repair, the tenant may:

(i) *claim damages, including the cost of having to take alternative accommodation until the repairs are done, plus a sum for mental distress and disappointment*
(This presupposes a successful court action. The problems with taking a landlord to court include the uncertainty, delay and expense involved.)

(ii) *ask the court to order the landlord to repair*
(But the court does not have to order the repair; whether they do is likely to depend on how seriously the lack of repairs affects the tenant's health, for example, and whether in their view financial damages would provide adequate compensation.)

(iii) *do the repairs himself and deduct the cost from future payments of rent*
(However, the tenant should proceed with caution, otherwise he might find the landlord seeking possession for rent arrears. First, he must be sure that there has been a breach of the covenant to repair and, secondly, warn the landlord that he intends to withhold the rent and use it to carry out the repairs. To be on the safe side, he should seek advice from a citizens advice bureau, housing aid or law centre.)

(iv) ask the local authority to require the landlord to carry out the repairs.

invoking Public Health and Housing Acts legislation to get repairs done

The person to contact is the local authority's environmental health inspector. If he finds premises in a state which would make them 'prejudicial to heath and a nuisance' with defects that need to be remedied urgently, the local authority may serve a notice on the landlord requiring him to carry out certain works. If the landlord does not start the repair work, or at least make clear his intention of starting the work within nine days, the local authority may carry out the work themselves. If the landlord says he intends to carry out the work but takes his time over it and does not start in a reasonable time, the local authority may also carry out the work themselves.

If a house is declared unfit for human habitation because of its bad state of repair (instability, dampness, faulty water supply, drainage and sanitary installations, lack of facilities for preparing food and disposing of waste water, etc) and work to bring it up to standard can be carried out at a reasonable cost, a notice can be served on the landlord by the local authority (under section 91 of the Housing Act

1957). This notice states what work is necessary to make the house fit and gives a reasonable time, not less than 21 days, in which the work should be finished.

If the local authority appears to be refusing to consider whether a house is unfit for habitation, the tenant can request a Justice of the Peace to visit the house (under the Housing Act 1957). If the JP feels that the house is unfit for human habitation, he can then make a complaint to the local authority; the local authority must then immediately inspect the house.

Where a house is not quite unfit for human habitation but in substantial disrepair, a notice may be served which specifies the work which the local authority thinks is necessary and states the time within which the work has to be done.

If a local authority feels that a landlord is not managing a house in multiple occupation properly they can (under the Housing Act 1961) require the landlord to carry out repairs and generally improve the management of the house. Where they consider it so bad that the only way of improving the conditions for the tenant is for the local authority to take over the management of the house in multiple occupation, the Housing Act 1964 can be invoked.

The Public Health Act 1936 (section 99) may be invoked by a tenant who feels that the local authority will not help to get repairs done to the house. The tenant can apply directly to the local magistrates' court for a summons to be served on the landlord. It is advisable to write to the landlord first, stating exactly what needs to be done and asking that the repairs should be done, before having a notice served on the landlord demanding that the work be carried out.

getting advice
The legislation exists but, in practice, enforcement may not be easy. SHAC (The London Housing Aid Centre, 189a Old Brompton Road, London SW5 0AR) suggests as sources of advice:

o **A housing aid centre:** Your council may have one or you can get a list from SHAC.

o **A local law centre:** The Law Centres Federation – telephone 01-387 8570, can tell you where your nearest one is.

○ **A neighbourhood advice centre** or other local community advice centre.

○ **A citizens advice bureau:** Look in the telephone directory to find the address of one in your area. Even if they cannot help they should be able to refer you to an agency which can.

grants
A free booklet published by the Department of the Environment and the Welsh Office *Home Improvement Grants*, a guide for home-owners, landlords and tenants, explains briefly what kinds of grant are available and the circumstances in which a tenant or landlord can apply. It says

"There are four separate kinds of grant
improvement grants are for major improvements, plus associated repairs and replacements

intermediate grants are for putting in missing standard amenities (inside toilet, bath, sink, washbasin, hot and cold water), plus associated repairs and replacements

repairs grants are for pre-1919 houses needing substantial and structural repairs

special grants (not available to tenants) are for putting in standard amenities and means of escape from fire in houses in multiple occupation, and for associated repairs and replacements.

Intermediate grants are mandatory, i.e. your local council cannot refuse you a grant provided you qualify. The other grants are normally given at the discretion of your local council."

The Consumer Publication *Householder's action guide* has a section on getting a grant and warns that 'grants which are at the discretion of the local authority could be suspended if the local authority does not have enough money. At present, the government is cutting down on these grants – some councils are still encouraging applications, others are not able to cope with demands.'

protection from harassment and the threat of eviction

It is an offence (under section 1 of the Protection from Eviction Act 1977) for anyone, including a landlord, to deprive a residential occupier of his premises or any part of the premises.

It is also an offence to do anything calculated to interfere with the peace or comfort of the residential occupier or members of his household, with intent to cause him to give up the premises or to stop him from exercising any of his rights and remedies in respect of the premises. It is similarly an offence intentionally to withhold services (for example, water, gas or electricity) that are reasonably required for the occupation of the premises.

Proving harassment is not easy; threats and abuse are obvious examples and so is cutting off of services (persistently, not just once) turning off the water or electricity, for example. Other examples of harassment would be changing the locks, letting gas or electricity meters jam up, throwing out belongings, allowing a pop group to rehearse in the next-door flat, writing threatening letters and issuing a 'notice to quit' without justification, withdrawing the rent book, or offering payment to the tenant to give up possession.

One of these acts can be sufficient to constitute harassment; there do not need to be several if the tenant's peace and comfort is interfered with so as to constitute a breach of the term implied in all tenancies (and expressly stated in some) that the tenant is allowed quiet enjoyment of the tenancy. Moreover, the act may be committed by someone acting on behalf of the landlord, not necessarily directly by the landlord. However, it must be proved that it was the intent of the harasser to force the occupier out or stop him from doing something he was entitled to do.

The landlord has not acted unlawfully if he can prove that he genuinely believed, and had reasonable cause to believe, that the occupier had ceased to live on the premises. A tenant or licensee who considers that he is being harassed should therefore state clearly that he intends to continue living at the premises and he should make sure that he does not stay away from the flat for long periods without leaving his everyday possessions there.

The protection applies to the 'residential occupier', that is a person occupying premises as a residence. Occupation may be under a contract or by virtue of any enactment or rule of law which gives him the right to remain in occupation or restricts the right of anyone else to recover possession of the premises. So, provided his residential occupation is lawful, the tenant or licensee is protected – but a trespasser or squatter is not.

invoking the courts
Illegal eviction is a criminal offence: a tenant should seek advice immediately if he thinks his landlord is trying to evict him illegally.

At present, the maximum penalty for contravening section 1 of the Protection Against Eviction Act is a fine of £1,000 and/or 6 months in prison (or if there has been a trial by jury, an unlimited fine and/or 2 years in prison). In addition, the court can order that compensation (of up to £2,000) be paid to the occupier if he suffered personal damage from the offence for which the landlord is convicted.

The occupier can also take civil action, by seeking an injunction against eviction or future harassment, or an order for reinstatement if he has been evicted, but it is advisable to do this with the help of a solicitor.

The SHAC booklet *Private tenants: protection from eviction* summarises what protection from eviction means and suggests that a tenant who is unsure of the degree of protection he has should contact a local law centre, or housing aid centre, neighbourhood advice centre or a solicitor for further advice.

regulated tenancies

The majority of residential lettings by private landlords are regulated tenancies under the Rent Act 1977 as amended by the Housing Act 1980. A regulated tenancy is mainly distinguished from others by where the landlord lives. If he lives in another dwelling (or is a property company) the tenancy is almost always regulated. In addition, for a tenancy to be regulated, the tenant must pay enough rent, but not too much, and the rateable value of the property must be below a set figure.

A regulated tenancy gives to a tenant the protection of controlled rent and security of tenure. Here is a summary of the more important consequences of a regulated tenancy.

○ The landlord cannot regain possession of the accommodation without a court order, and the court may only grant an order in prescribed circumstances.

○ When the tenant dies, the tenancy will usually pass to a member of his family who has been living in the dwelling.

○ The court may order the transfer of a regulated tenancy from one spouse to another when a decree of judicial separation or divorce is granted, or at any time afterwards.

○ The landlord and the tenant, together or separately (and also the local authority) can apply to the rent officer for a fair rent to be registered.

○ If no rent is registered, the parties are free to agree a rent, provided certain formalities are observed. There is no limit on the rent the parties can agree.

○ If a fair rent is registered, that is the maximum rent the landlord can charge until it is properly changed.

○ The tenant has rights in respect of any variable service charge he pays.

Regulated tenants also are able to enforce the rights theoretically available to all tenants, for example rights to repair, or to quiet enjoyment of their home, without risking eviction as a result of their actions.

definition

The definition of a regulated tenancy has three component parts. There must be:

(i) a dwelling-house

(ii) which is let

(iii) as a separate dwelling.

(i) a dwelling-house
'Dwelling-house' has been interpreted very widely by the courts. It includes a house or part of a house, a cottage, bungalow, maisonette or flat, a single room (for example a bedroom or bed-sit), even a beach-hut. Two flats let together as one dwelling may constitute a dwelling-house, and so may a house and an adjacent cottage which are let together. The premises may be furnished or unfurnished.

(ii) which is let
There must be a tenancy: the relationship of landlord and tenant must exist. A licence to occupy cannot be a regulated tenancy. Thus lodgers, caretakers and employees who have to occupy accommodation because of their job are excluded. It does not matter how the tenancy was created, whether by deed, written agreement or by word of mouth, nor whether it is a periodic tenancy or a tenancy for a fixed term.

(iii) as a separate dwelling

It must be intended at the time of the letting that the tenant should live in the accommodation. If the letting is for some other purpose, a shop for instance, then it is not a regulated tenancy. One tenant who used to sleep in his antique shop, failed in his claim to be a regulated tenant. The letting was for the purpose of his antiques business.

The accommodation must be let as a single unit. This normally means that the tenant must be able to sleep, cook and eat there. It seems that washing is a secondary aspect of living – the fact that a tenant has to share bathroom facilities with others does not prevent a regulated tenancy from arising. One dwelling-house may comprise several single units, let separately; but if all the accommodation in the dwelling-house is shared, there is no letting of a separate dwelling. Furthermore, two self-contained units (for example two flats) may constitute a separate dwelling if let as such.

exceptions

The letting will not be a regulated tenancy if one (or more) of the following twelve exceptions applies:

   (i) If the rateable value of the property is above the rateable value limits laid down by the Rent Act 1977. The way in which the limits are defined by section 4 of the Act is complicated, but broadly speaking a property will be within the rateable value limits if its present rateable value is £1,500 or less in Greater London, or £750 or less elsewhere. If the present rateable value of a property is higher than this, it may still come within the rateable value limits if its rateable value on the valuation list which expired on 31st March 1973 was £600 or less in Greater London, or £300 or less elsewhere.

   (ii) If no rent is payable, or the rent is a low rent. The rent payable under the tenancy must be not less than ⅔ of the rateable value on 'the appropriate day'. 'The appropriate day' is either 23 March 1965 if the property was rated at that time or, if not, the date on which it became rated. In this context, rent means the actual rent payable, without deduction for rates and taxes paid by the landlord. Long leaseholders (that is, whose lease is for 21 years or more) are usually excluded from being regulated tenants because they pay little or no rent; their payments for rates, services, maintenance or insurance are not counted for this purpose.

A tenant can lose the protection of the Rent Act through a change in the terms of his tenancy, for example if a landlord offers a regulated tenant a new lease at a low rent, and he accepts.

(iii) If part of the tenant's dwelling-house is licensed for the sale of intoxicating liquor for consumption on the premises. A publican letting a flat above his pub, however, can do so on a regulated tenancy.

(iv) If the rent includes payment for board or attendance. As far as attendance is concerned, the exclusion only operates if the payment for it forms a substantial part of the rent.

Board means 'prepared food served on the premises'. An early morning cup of tea would not count; continental breakfast probably would. Landlords sometimes go to great pains to bring themselves within this exception – perhaps spending the early hours of the morning leaving plates of steaming eggs and bacon on the doorsteps of numerous tenants.

Attendance means 'services personal to the tenant' and would include cleaning rooms and washing linen, but not the cleaning of communal parts, such as entrance hall and stairways.

(v) If the letting is by a university, college or polytechnic to one of its students, or by some other body specified by regulation. The bodies are all educational institutions and foundations specifically established to provide accommodation. This is relevant to students and the people who rent from these bodies while the accommodation is not required for students.

(vi) If the purpose of the letting is to confer on the tenant the right to occupy the dwelling-house for a holiday. If the agreement contains a statement that it is a holiday letting, it would be up to the tenant to prove to the court that the expressed purpose is a sham.

(vii) If the property is let for business or mixed residential and business purposes.

(viii) If the landlord is a local authority, a new town development corporation, a housing association registered with the Housing Corporation, a housing trust which is a registered charity, the Housing Corporation, the Commission for the New Towns or the Development Board for Rural Wales.

(ix) If the landlord is a government department. (Lettings by the Crown, however, are not excluded from being regulated tenancies unless they fall within one of the other exceptions.)

(x) If the letting is an assured tenancy.

(xi) If the tenancy was granted after 14 August 1974 by a resident landlord. A 'resident landlord' is one who lives in the same house or flat as the tenant and has done so from the time the tenant moved in. Living in the same block of flats (as against in the same flat) would not make him a resident landlord. Although a resident landlord must show that he was resident in the property at the time of the letting, he may have more than one home and need not occupy any of them continuously. But he must always intend to return and use the property as a home and show visible signs of that intention, such as leaving clothes there.

Before 1974, the distinction was between furnished and unfurnished tenancies, rather than resident and non-resident landlords. Furnished tenancies were excepted from protection. It may be necessary to decide whether a tenancy created before August 1974 was furnished or unfurnished, because if it was unfurnished, it will still be a regulated tenancy even though there is a resident landlord.

(xii) If the landlord is not resident but shares living accommodation with the tenant (a kitchen or sitting-room; sharing a w.c. or bathroom does not count).

disputes

If there is any doubt whether or not a regulated tenancy has been created, either the landlord or the tenant may apply to the county court for a declaration as to the status of the letting. A tenant would be wise to seek legal advice before embarking on this. If the court finds against him, not only will he be putting his home at risk, but will incur court costs. It may be better for him to await possession action by the landlord and then attempt to establish a regulated tenancy as part of the defence.

protected and statutory tenancies

A regulated tenancy may be either protected or statutory. It is protected while the original agreement, written or oral, is in existence. When the protected tenancy comes to an end, provided the tenant goes on living in the accommodation, what is known as a statutory tenancy will arise on the same terms and conditions as originally agreed (in so far as they are consistent with a statutory tenancy).

This statutory tenancy confers no interest in land on the tenant; it is merely a personal right to remain in occupation and will last only as long as the tenant remains in residence. As a consequence, the tenant cannot normally assign (that is, sell) or sub-let the whole of the premises.

This does not mean that a statutory tenant can never leave his home, and it is recognised that a person can have more than one home. *'The tenant cannot be compelled to spend 24 hours in all weathers under his own roof for 365 days in the year. Clearly, the tenant of a London house who spends his weekends in the country or his long vacation in Scotland, does not necessarily cease to be in occupation.'*

Generally speaking, the tenant must at times use the accommodation as his home and, if away, always intend to return. Thus a tenant, with a house in the country, who stayed in his flat twice a week, but rarely ate a meal there, succeeded in his claim to a statutory tenancy. In another case, however, a statutory tenant of a flat went to live with his girlfriend although he left clothes and furniture in the flat, he never returned there at night. Very occasionally he used the flat during the day to work. He lost his statutory tenancy.

Where either a husband or wife is entitled to occupy accommodation by virtue of a statutory tenancy, as long as the other spouse is there that counts as occupation by the tenant, for the purposes of keeping the statutory tenancy alive. The landlord cannot refuse to accept rent from whichever spouse is in occupation.

successors

On the death of the original tenant, whether still protected or statutory, the tenancy is automatically transferred as a statutory tenancy to a 'first successor' and on the death of the first successor to a 'second successor'. When the second successor dies, the statutory tenancy comes to an end.

who is the 'first successor'?

Provided the tenant's husband or wife was living in the property before the tenant died, he or she will be the first successor. If this does not apply, the first successor can be any member of the tenant's family (including adopted children and a so-called 'common law' wife or husband) who was living with the tenant during the six months preceding his or her death. If more than one relative qualifies, and succession cannot be decided between the relatives by agreement, the county court can be asked to decide.

A 'second successor' succeeds in exactly the same way, namely the first successor's surviving spouse, then a resident relative.

an anomaly
A protected tenant owns an interest in land which on his death will pass in the normal way to the person entitled under his will or intestacy. But that person's entitlement to the protected tenancy may be suspended, possibly for the lifetime of two successors, if a transmitted statutory tenancy is claimed by a resident spouse or relative.

Example: In 1970, Paul Turner, a widower, got a flat with a twenty year lease that will come to an end in 1990. He lives there with his sister Sarah. In 1985 he dies without having made a will. Under the intestacy rules his property, which includes the lease of the flat, goes to his daughter Diana. But Sarah can, and does, stay on – as the successor. Her niece Nora moves in with her, and on Sarah's death Nora becomes the second successor to the by then statutory tenancy. Only on Nora's death would Diana's entitlement become effective but not if the period of the original lease has come to an end (i.e. after 1990).

divorced and separated spouses
Under the Matrimonial Homes Act 1983, the court has power on granting a decree of divorce, nullity, or judicial separation, or at any later time, to make an order transferring a protected or statutory tenancy from one spouse to the other. This jurisdiction does not extend to unmarried couples.

getting vacant possession

A landlord cannot get vacant possession from a regulated tenant unless, if the tenancy is still protected, he ends it in the proper manner and obtains a possession order from the court. For this, he must establish one of the grounds for possession set out in the Rent Act.

ending a protected tenancy

If the tenancy can be ended by notice to quit, either because there is an express term to this effect or because the tenancy is a periodic one, at least four weeks' notice in writing must be given to the tenant. The period of notice will have to be longer if the lease so requires, or if the tenancy period is for more than four weeks. A notice to quit a periodic tenancy must expire at the end of a complete period of the tenancy (for example at the end of the week, if weekly) unless the tenancy agreement states otherwise.

notice to quit

A notice to quit must contain the following prescribed information (in the recommended form of words):

'1. *If the tenant does not leave the dwelling, the landlord must get an order for possession from the court before the tenant can lawfully be evicted. The landlord cannot apply for such an order before the notice to quit has run out.*

'2. *A tenant who does not know if he has any right to remain in possession after a notice to quit runs out or is otherwise unsure of his rights, can obtain advice from a solicitor. Help with all or part of the cost of legal advice and assistance may be available under the Legal Aid Scheme. He should also be able to obtain information from a Citizens Advice Bureau, a Housing Aid Centre, a Rent Officer or a Rent Tribunal Office.'*

Standard *Notice to Quit a Dwelling* forms are available from law stationers.

When a protected tenant receives a notice to quit, he does not have to get out there and then. He does not need to leave unless and until the landlord has obtained a possession order from the court.

no notice to quit

It is unusual for a lease for a fixed term to require also a notice to quit; it comes to an end automatically on the specified date and cannot be ended sooner. After that date, a statutory tenancy arises, and the landlord can apply to the court for a possession order. A notice to quit is never necessary in the case of a statutory tenancy. But the landlord would need a court order for possession before the tenant needs to move out.

obtaining a court order for possession

Most of the statutory grounds for possession are called 'cases' which are either discretionary or mandatory. There are ten mandatory cases, and ten discretionary ones but one of these (case vii) was abolished by the Housing Act 1980.

discretionary grounds for possession

These are listed in Part I of Schedule 15 of the Rent Act 1977. There are ten (but one has been abolished by the Housing Act 1980). The court may grant an order for possession if it thinks it reasonable to do so in any one of the following cases:

CASE I
The tenant has not paid the rent or is in breach of one of his other obligations in the tenancy agreement – for example, to repair. The court can suspend the operation of a possession order on conditions, for example that the tenant pays off all arrears of rent, or does the necessary repairs.

(The order to pay off the arrears should only be made if it would not cause exceptional hardship to the tenant; tenants on supplementary benefit can argue that exceptional hardship will be caused if they are placed below supplementary benefit level or, at any rate, the level which the DHSS is allowed to deduct from their benefit to pay off arrears where rent is paid direct.)

CASE II
The tenant has caused a nuisance or annoyance to neighbours (not necessarily adjoining but in the near vicinity) *or has been convicted of using the premises for illegal or immoral purposes.*

One landlord got a possession order under the nuisance part of case II against a tenant who adamantly refused to mow the lawn and let the grass grow uncontrolled. In general, the nuisance must be proved to be serious and persistent.

CASE III
The tenant has damaged the property or allowed it to deteriorate (except for fair wear and tear).

CASE IV
The tenant has damaged furniture that was provided by the landlord (except for fair wear and tear).

CASE V
The tenant gave notice to quit (but subsequently changed his mind) and in consequence of the notice the landlord has contracted to sell or let the property. The landlord would need to show that the tenant not leaving would cause him financial loss.

CASE VI
The tenant has assigned or sub-let the whole of the property without the landlord's consent. This is only appropriate to a protected tenancy; a statutory tenant who assigns or sub-lets the whole of the property puts the tenant outside the protection of the Rent Act.

CASE VIII
The tenant was an employee of the landlord and the landlord now reasonably requires the accommodation for a new employee.

CASE IX
The landlord reasonably requires the property as a home for himself or member of his immediate family. To grant an order for possession under this case, the court must be satisfied that greater hardship would be caused by refusing the order than by granting it.

The court may make an order for future possession, as it did where a 62-year old landlord wanted possession of a tenanted cottage so that she would have somewhere to live on her mother's imminent death.

But the landlord cannot use case IX if he had bought the property after 1974 with a furnished sitting tenant in it, or had bought it after 1965 with any other sitting tenant in it.

CASE X
The tenant has charged a sub-tenant a higher rent than that allowed by the Rent Act.

suitable alternative accommodation
The court may also make an order for possession at its discretion (without the landlord having to prove any of the cases) if it is satisfied that suitable alternative accommodation is available to the tenant, or will be available to him when the order for possession takes effect.

There are two ways in which a landlord can show the existence of suitable alternative accommodation. Firstly, he can produce a certificate from a local housing authority certifying that they are providing the alternative accommodation. Local authorities rarely give such certificates. Secondly, he can find and offer alternative accommodation himself. This accommodation will be suitable if:

   (i) it gives the tenant equal or equivalent security of tenure; *and*

(ii) it is reasonably convenient as regard the tenant's and his or her family's place of work;
and

(iii) the rent and size of the accommodation are that which a local authority or court would consider suitable for the needs of the tenant and his or her family;
and

(iv) where appropriate, similar or suitable furniture is provided;
and

(v) the character of the property is suitable to the tenant's and his or her family's needs.

It can be very difficult for a landlord to show that this last requirement has been satisfied if the tenant objects. But it has recently been considered by the court. A retired couple were statutory tenants of The Grange, a period country house with a large number of rooms, servants' quarters, outbuildings, stables, a large garden and about one and a half acres of land. The landlords bought, for £52,000, a four-bedroomed modern detached house with a garden and garage near to The Grange, and offered it as alternative accommodation to the couple. The offer was refused. The court granted an order for possession. In assessing the suitability of alternative accommodation, the court has to look at the tenant's needs, not his particular wishes and desires. The house clearly satisfied the couple's housing needs, if not their wishes.

The court will also grant an order for possession if the property is statutorily defined as being overcrowded under the Housing Act 1957.

mandatory grounds for possession

These are listed in Part II of Schedule 15 to the Rent Act. There are also ten. If the landlord establishes any of the grounds detailed in cases XI to XX, the court is obliged to grant him a possession order, irrespective of whether it thinks it reasonable to do so.

The landlord must have given 'notice in writing to the tenant that possession might be recovered under this case', no later than the start of the tenancy (before the grant of the tenancy, in the case of a shorthold). But this requirement may be waived and a possession order granted by the court in cases xi, xii, xix and xx provided it thinks it just and equitable to do so.

There is a special procedure enabling landlords to get possession quickly under cases xi to xx. The county court office can advise on how to do this (and will help applicants to complete forms and explain exactly the steps to be followed). A tenant faced with such proceedings has to act fast: the period between his receiving the court papers and the hearing need not be as long as the usual 21 days – it may, in some cases, be as little as 7 days.

Once a mandatory order for possession is made, it cannot be postponed for more than 14 days except on the grounds of exceptional hardship.

The tenant will have been informed before he took the tenancy that the landlord might mandatorily recover possession under the appropriate case. The county court summons will also state this. The tenant has to get out within 14 days or, if exceptional hardship, six weeks. Exceptional hardship is a question of fact in each case – for example, a family with several small children would take a little longer than two weeks to find somewhere to live.

Here are the ten mandatory cases:

CASE XI *returning owner-occupiers*
Case xi was designed to enable a person to let his home temporarily. Provided the landlord lived in the accommodation before letting it and, from the start of that tenancy and previous ones, gave written notice to the tenant that possession might be recovered under case xi, the court will order the tenant to move out if it is satisfied regarding one of the following:

(1) the owner-occupier or any member of his family who was living with him when he last occupied the accommodation, wishes to live in it; or

(2) the owner-occupier has died and a member of his family who was living with him when he last occupied the accommodation (or another house) wishes to live in it; or

(3) the owner-occupier has died and the person who has inherited the property either wants to live in it or sell it with vacant possession; or

(4) the property is subject to a mortgage and the lender wishes to exercise his power of sale (for example because repayments have not been made); or

(5) the owner-occupier wants to sell the property with vacant possession in order to buy a home nearer his work.

And if it considers it just and equitable, the court can still grant an order for possession, even though the owner did not live continuously in the property immediately before the letting and/or did not serve the proper notice.

In practice, it can be safer even where case xi would apply, for the landlord to retain out of the lease a bedroom in the house and a right of access to it, so that if he returns from his absence abroad, say, he can still at least have access to a room in the house while the court proceedings are going ahead.

An 'owner-occupier' does not have to be a freeholder: a tenant who is entitled to sub-let the whole of his home under his agreement can also use case xi.

The Department of the Environment Housing booklet No 5 *Letting your Home or Retirement Home* is a guide for home owners and servicemen who want to let their homes temporarily.

CASE XII *retirement homes*
This case can be used by people who let a home to which they plan to retire. The owner must intend to live in the accommodation when he retires from regular employment and must have given the tenant notice in writing on or before the start of the tenancy that possession might be required under case xii. If the owner has previously let the property, it must also have been under case xii. The court must order the tenant to give up possession if it is satisfied that:

(1) the owner has retired from regular employment and wants to use the property as a retirement home; or

(2) the owner has died and a member of his family who was living with him at the time of his death, wants to live in the property; or

(3) the owner has died and a person who has inherited the property either wants to live in it or sell it with vacant possession; or

(4) the property is mortgaged and the lender wishes to sell it with vacant possession.

The court may waive the requirement that proper notice must be served or that any previous letting must have been under case XII.

CASE XIII *out of 'holiday season' lettings*
This case deals with the problem of what to do with holiday homes out of season. If the home was let for a fixed term of 8 months or less having been let for a holiday during the previous twelve months, the landlord must be granted a possession order.

Suppose A has a seaside bungalow near Great Yarmouth which he lets out to holidaymakers during the season. From May to October he let the bungalow to Mr. and Mrs. X on a genuine holiday let. No one seems to want to spend money on a seaside holiday there during the winter, and instead of leaving the bungalow empty for the winter months, A decides to let Fred, the local postman, rent it. As long as he does not grant Fred a lease for longer than 8 months, he will be able to get a (mandatory) possession order from the court to get Fred out again, because the bungalow was genuinely let for a holiday during the 12 months prior to the lease to Fred.

CASE XIV *out of 'student term' lettings*
This is similar to case XIII. It allows the accommodation owned by educational institutions to be let while it is not required for student use. The accommodation must have been let for a fixed term of 12 months or less, having been let to students during the previous twelve months.

CASE XV *clergy lettings*
The court must order possession if the accommodation was intended for a clergyman but was temporarily let to an ordinary tenant.

CASE XVI *farmworker lettings*
Similarly, possession will be granted to a farmer who lets property that is usually occupied by a farm worker to an ordinary tenant on a temporary basis.

CASE XVII *farmhouse lettings*
This applies where a landlord requires a farmhouse not previously occupied by a farm manager following amalgamation proposals.

CASE XVIII *farm manager lettings*
This case covers the situation where the accommodation was previously occupied by a farm manager or his widow and has been let temporarily to an ordinary tenant.

CASE XIX *shorthold tenancies*
(Shorthold tenancies are dealt with separately on pages 57–61.)

CASE XX *lettings by servicemen*
This case is similar to cases XI and XII: where a person was a member of the armed forces when he bought and let the property, and the tenant and any previous tenant was given notice on or before the start of the tenancy that possession might be recovered under case XX, the court must grant an order for possession if it is satisfied that:

(1) the serviceman wants to live in the property; *or*

(2) a member of his family who was living with him at the time of his death, now wants to live in the property; *or*

(3) a person who has inherited the property either wishes to live in it or sell it with vacant possession; *or*

(4) the serviceman needs to sell the property with vacant possession to buy a home nearer his work; *or*

(5) the property is mortgaged and the lender wishes to exercise his power to sell it with vacant possession.

tenant ending a regulated tenancy

How a tenant can do this depends on whether the regulated tenancy is protected or statutory.

If the tenancy is still protected and is a

(a) *periodic tenancy* – the tenant must give the landlord at least four weeks' notice to quit, expiring at the end of a complete period of the tenancy (for example the end of a week if the tenancy is weekly). The notice must be in writing but no special form is required. If the tenancy agreement provides for a longer period of notice to be given, the tenant will have to comply with this.

(b) *fixed term tenancy* – the tenant may only end a fixed term tenancy prematurely if either the agreement or the landlord allows him to do so.

If the tenancy has become statutory, the tenant must give the landlord at least four weeks' notice to quit in writing, but more if the terms of the original agreement require longer notice to be given. Where the original tenancy was for a fixed term, the tenant must give at least three months' notice in writing. Again, the landlord may agree to the tenant leaving without giving notice.

private (non-statutory) agreement

The landlord and the tenant may come to an agreement that the tenant should vacate the premises in return for some financial compensation. Any such agreement, while not being illegal, would be unenforceable. So, any such agreed payment would need to be handed to the tenant in cash (or by way of banker's draft) as the tenant is leaving. The tenant will obviously not leave unless he is certain to get the money, whereas the landlord will not part with the money unless he is sure of getting vacant possession.

In some cases, substantial payments are made because the property is far more valuable to the landlord vacant than occupied. Precisely what this increase in value is and how it is to be split between the landlord and the tenant is open to negotiation between them, but the benefit to both parties makes an agreement possible.

rent control

Security of tenure is not the only advantage of a regulated tenancy. The amount of rent the tenant has to pay may be limited to what is known as a 'fair rent'.

A fair rent is one assessed by a rent officer or, on appeal, a rent assessment committee, in accordance with the rules laid down in the Rent Act. Once assessed, the rent is entered in the rent register which is kept by the rent officer and is open to public inspection, free of charge. By looking at rents registered for similar dwellings in the area, a landlord and a tenant can get an idea of the fair rent attributable to their accommodation.

getting a fair rent registered

Either the landlord or the tenant of any regulated tenancy, or both of them together, or the local authority, may apply to the local rent officer for a fair rent to be registered. The address of the rent officer is in the telephone directory.

Application is made on form RR1, available on request from the rent officer, law centres, citizens advice bureaux, housing aid centres. The form is easily completed and asks, amongst other things, for details of the landlord and tenant, a description of the premises and the terms of the tenancy (a copy of any written agreement should be included), whether or not services and furniture are provided and whether a fair rent has been previously registered for the premises.

The rent (exclusive of rates) which the applicant seeks to have registered must be entered on the form. If no rent is specified, the rent officer cannot deal with the application. If the applicant is the landlord, a copy of the application is sent to the tenant, and vice versa.

The parties are usually asked if they wish to meet the rent officer for a consultation. If so, a meeting will be arranged for a few weeks hence. Shortly before the meeting, the rent officer may inspect the premises, accompanied by the parties if they so desire.

The rent officer then decides on a fair rent. The Rent Act requires that in doing so he should have regard to the character, state of repair and locality of the dwelling and if the tenancy is furnished the quality and condition of the furniture. He often starts by looking at the fair rents already registered for similar accommodation in the area. He should disregard any value arising from a shortage of rented accommodation in the area. The value of any improvements made or paid for by the tenant should also be disregarded. The personal and financial circumstances of the landlord and tenant must also be ignored. The resulting fair rent will be registered about six to eight weeks after the initial application was received. Both parties will be sent a copy of the registration sheet, together with copies of the rent officer's papers on the case and notes outlining the effect of the registration.

The Organisation of Private Tenants (19 Highbury Place, London N5 1QT) jointly with the Paddington Federation of Tenants and Residents Association (59 Star Street, London W2) has published *A pocket guide to rent registration* (price 40p) which sets out the procedure step by step.

the service element

A registered rent reflects the cost of any services provided by the landlord, for instance, porterage and cleaning. Details of the cost of any services have to be entered on the application form by whoever is making the application, and can be challenged and must be substantiated if the tenant or rent officer so requires. If a 'fixed' fair rent is registered, such part of it as is attributable to services is noted separately (unless it is less than 5% of the total rent) and so is any increase in the cost of services since the previous rent. The amount of any increase called the 'service element' of the registered rent is not subject to the rules about phasing the increase.

Often a tenancy agreement provides that the landlord may vary any service charge payable. If the rent officer approves this provision, he will register a rent which reflects, but does not detail, the current cost of services, and state that the fair rent is 'variable'. This means that a landlord can recover the actual amount expended on services for any particular period of time. How this amount is split among different flat owners in a block depends on the agreement between the landlord and the flat owners. Sometimes the charge is split pro rata according to the size of each flat, sometimes it is just split equally. Any extra service charge is collected in the same way.

The Housing Act 1980 gives to a tenant who has to pay a variable service charge the right to obtain a summary of the costs on which any service charge was calculated, to inspect the accounts and receipts on which the summary is based, and to challenge the charge on the grounds that the standard or cost of any item was unreasonable or that it was unreasonably incurred. Further, if the tenant is liable to contribute towards the cost of repairs, he has the right to be consulted before the landlord carries out any repair work. In certain cases of more major repairs, the landlord must obtain at least two estimates for consideration by the tenant, one of which must be from a person, firm or company wholly independent of the landlord.

The Department of the Environment's booklet *Service Charges in Flats* gives an outline of the provisions in the Housing Act 1980 regarding variable service charges.

no rates element

A registered rent does not include rates. If the landlord pays the rates, he cannot recover them from the tenant unless the tenancy is statutory or the tenancy agreement so provides. In any other case, the landlord will have to wait until the protected tenancy has ended before he can begin to charge for rates. A periodic protected tenancy can be ended by the landlord serving a *Notice of Increase of Rates.*

The length of notice must be the same length as a notice to quit. When the notice has expired, the periodic protected tenancy ends and a statutory tenancy comes into being (which is why in the case of a registered rent the landlord can charge for rates, but the notice cannot be backdated).

certificate of fair rent

Prospective landlords can discover what a fair rent for their premises would be by applying for a certificate of fair rent. New developers and landlords intending to carry out improvements to tenanted or untenanted premises often avail themselves of this procedure.

Form CFRI has to be used, available from the rent officer. It requires similar details as form RRI and asks for the ground of application – whether new dwellings will be created by building or conversion, whether improvements will be made, and whether premises will be let on a regulated tenancy. The rent the landlord wishes to have registered must be specified. The landlord and any tenant can consult with the rent officer and the premises are normally inspected.

An objection can be made to the fair rent which the rent officer proposes to insert in a certificate. If no objection is received (the tenant, if any, is given 14 days to object) the certificate is issued. When the property is let, or the improvements have been carried out as proposed, the landlord may apply to the rent officer to have the fair rent in the certificate registered. The application must be made within two years of the date the certificate is issued.

objection

If the landlord or the tenant is dissatisfied with the rent registered, he may (within 28 days of receiving notification of the registration) ask the rent officer by letter or in person to refer the matter to a tribunal called the rent assessment committee. A committee is normally made up of three people: a layman, a valuer and a lawyer who acts as chairman. They take a new look at the facts and assess a rent for the premises which they deem fair at the time of their decision.

An objection cannot be made if:

○ a joint application was made by the landlord and the tenant and the rent officer determined, without further consultation, that the rent specified in the application was a fair one; or

○ the landlord had obtained a certificate of fair rent and the rent registered was the same as the certificate.

When the committee has received an objection, the party objecting is sent a printed explanation (on form RR102) of how his case will be dealt with. Next, a letter (known as RR7H) is sent to both parties asking them whether they wish to make oral or written representations. The letter may also give the date, time and place of the hearing if it has been decided to call one. There is a time limit for replying to RR7H, usually 7 days. Any of the rent officer's papers on the case which were not sent to the parties previously will accompany the letter. At this stage, the committee may ask either party to supply further information. There is a fine if this is not done within 14 days.

If no hearing has been requested, both parties are given the opportunity to comment on each other's written representations. The committee nearly always inspects the premises before making a decision.

the hearing
If a hearing has been requested, or is ordered by the committee, the parties will be given about 10 days' notice of its date, time and venue, by standard letter (RR8). Hearings are open to the public. The parties may speak for themselves or get someone else to represent them (not necessarily a solicitor).

The course of the hearing depends on who attends. The committee can go ahead with the hearing even though one of the parties does not turn up, provided they are satisfied that sufficient warning was given. The applicant will be called first. If he is the landlord, he will be asked to state his rent proposals and the tenant is given the opportunity to question him. Then the tenant will be asked to present his case, and the landlord is allowed to question him. The committee may also question the parties and witnesses may be asked to speak.

The object of a hearing (and also written representations) is to acquaint the committee fully with the arguments of both sides.

Although the idea of appealing to a tribunal is daunting to most laymen, they should not be afraid. The chairman of the committee is likely to be helpful. He says when the parties should speak and when they should question and is willing to answer any reasonable questions himself.

Both parties should state what they think the rent should be, and why. Relevant points may include the size, age and locality of the dwelling, its state of repair and any furniture and services provided. The shortage of rented accommodation in the area will not be considered by the committee, and the financial and personal circumstances of the parties are irrelevant – for example, where a tenant cannot take advantage of facilities offered and included in rent (such as upkeep of lift for ground floor tenant or use of tennis court for 86-year-old granny). The idea is to be fair to both parties – to assess what would be an objective fair rent for the premises (therefore the scarcity value, which benefits a landlord, is also disregarded).

The committee will confirm the rent officer's figure if it appears to them to be fair. If not, they will determine a fair rent themselves which may be higher or lower, fixed or variable (if the lease allows for a variation). They sometimes give their decision at the hearing but more usually it is communicated through the post (using form RR9). The committee need not, and do not, give reasons for their decision unless one of the parties asks them to do so before the hearing. Their decision is also sent to the rent officer. He then either marks in the register that the rent is confirmed or registers the new rent.

There is a right to appeal to the High Court against a committee's decision on a point of law; but the High Court cannot determine a fair rent for the premises.

It is important to realise that on an objection by either party, the rent can be increased or decreased and both the landlord and the tenant should give careful consideration whether an objection should be made, since either of them may end up worse off than they would have been if they had not made the objection.

withdrawal of objection
When a matter has been referred to a rent assessment committee, either party may withdraw his objection if the other party and the committee agree. However, the committee can continue with the case if they think it is against the public interest to withdraw.

the effect of registering a fair rent

Once a fair rent is registered, this is the maximum rent that the landlord can ask to be paid as from the effective date of the registration. For a rent assessed by the rent officer, the effective date is normally the date of registration; for one that has been determined by the rent assessment committee, it is the date of their decision. A registration remains in force, notwithstanding a change of tenant, until a new application for registration is made or until the registration is cancelled.

If the fair rent is lower than the rent previously paid by the tenant, the landlord must reduce the rent from the effective date. If the tenant has been paying a higher rent than that already registered, which sometimes happens when a new tenant is unaware that a fair rent has been registered for the premises, he can recover overpayments made in the past two years.

phasing the increase
If the fair rent is greater than that currently being charged, the increase must be phased and cannot be made all at once. Half the increase plus any 'service element' (that is the difference between present and previous amounts attributable to providing services) is payable straightaway, the other half becomes due one year later.

A registered rent is exclusive of rates, so the previous rent limit should, for phasing purposes, also be exclusive. Since many unregistered rents are inclusive, a sum for rates may need to be deducted before calculating phasing.

Unless the tenancy is still protected and the agreement allows for increases, the landlord must serve a prescribed *Notice of Increase* (available from law stationers) on the tenant before he can claim either part of the increased rent, but one notice can cover both phases of the increase.

If the tenancy is protected, and the agreement does not allow for increases, the landlord cannot start charging the fair rent until he has ended the tenancy. (He will most probably not be able to do this if the tenancy is for a fixed term, but must wait until the term expires.) A periodic tenancy is usually ended by a notice to quit; to save the landlord having to serve both notices, a notice of increase can serve two purposes. Provided it is for the same length as the notice to quit, it ends the protected tenancy and enables the landlord to charge the first half of the increased rent.

The only way in which a registered rent may be varied is by applying for a new rent to be registered or for the present one to be cancelled.

applying for a new rent to be registered
A new application for registration cannot be made until two years have elapsed from the date when the last registration took effect, except where:

○ a landlord submits an application for re-registration three months before that date (but any new registration will not take effect until the two years are up); or

○ a joint application is made by the landlord and tenant; or

○ there has been a material change in the condition of the dwelling or in the terms of the tenancy and the registered rent is no longer a fair rent.

cancellation

The landlord and the tenant can apply jointly to have a registered rent cancelled. The application should be made on form RR103 and two years must have elapsed since the effective date of the last registration. The parties must have agreed a new rent and a copy of their rent agreement (which must comply with the rules) should accompany the application. One term of the agreement must be that the landlord cannot end the tenancy (except for non-payment of rent or breach of any other covenant) within 12 months of the application for cancellation. The rent officer can only cancel if he is satisfied that the rent payable under the proposed agreement is not higher than the previous fair rent. There is no right of appeal from his decision. If he decides not to cancel, the registered rent continues in force.

Once the rent is cancelled, the parties can make further rent agreements. A cancellation stops neither party from later applying to the rent officer to determine a fair rent.

A tenant may be tempted to participate in an application for cancellation if he suspects that the landlord is offering him a lower than fair rent, even though this will cancel his regulated status (with its inherent protection).

A landlord may apply for a cancellation on his own, if two years have elapsed since the effective date of the last registration and the premises are not currently let to a regulated tenant. The prescribed form is form RR104.

When a new tenancy is granted and there was no fair rent registered in respect of the property during a previous tenancy, the parties can agree on whatever rent they choose. Once they have agreed a figure for rent, that figure can only be increased if the tenancy is still contractual and the agreement so provides or, where the agreement does not allow for increases, by a formal rent agreement. Such an agreement must be in writing, signed by both parties and state 'in characters not less conspicuous than those used in any other part of the agreement' that the tenant's security of tenure under the Rent Act will not be affected if he refused to enter into the agreement, that in any event he may apply at any time to the rent officer for a rent to be registered and that if the increase had been determined on application for registration, then the increase would have been phased.

Housing booklet No 7 *Regulated Tenancies* (issued by the Department of the Environment and Welsh Office) concentrates on explanations of fair rents and security of tenure.

miscellaneous points about regulated tenancies

premiums and associated payments

It is a criminal offence to require or receive a premium or 'key money' as a condition of a grant or renewal of a regulated tenancy or the transfer of it to a new tenant. On conviction, the landlord may be ordered to repay the money to the tenant. The payment does not have to be made to the landlord to constitute an illegal premium; it can be made to his agent or to a tenant who is transferring the tenancy.

A premium includes any payment in addition to rent, for example the excess over a reasonable price for furniture. A landlord may, however, take a deposit or 'danger money' from a tenant, furnished or unfurnished, provided it is not more than one-sixth of the annual rent and is reasonable in relation to the tenant's potential liability.

It is also an offence to require a tenant to pay rent in advance of the rental period it covers (suppose it is a monthly tenancy, the landlord cannot demand December's rent in November but he can ask for it on 1 December) or to pay rent more than six months in advance. The tenant is entitled to recover any rent so paid.

It is not an offence for the landlord to pay the tenant for the surrender of the lease, although any agreement or contract to this effect will be unenforceable.

rent books

The use of a rent book is widespread but the duty on the landlord to provide one is limited; he need only do so where rent is payable weekly.

A rent book is useful because of the information it must contain. It must state the name and address of the landlord and his agent, the address of the premises, the rent and rates payable by the occupier, and the terms and conditions of the tenancy, explain to the tenant his right to security of tenure and rent control, and mention the existence of local authority housing benefit (previously rent allowance) schemes. Rent books can be bought from law stationers.

Failure to provide a rent book is a criminal offence punishable by a fine (a maximum of £50 for a first offence, and £100 for subsequent offences) but it does not affect the right of the landlord to recover rent properly due to him.

A rent book is a convenient way of bringing to tenants' attention information about their rights under the Rent Act, and it also provides a record of the terms of the tenancy, so reducing the possibility of disputes. The rationale behind the rule that a rent book needs to be provided only where rent is payable weekly is that weekly tenancies are invariably oral, longer tenancies are in writing and therefore do not require the protection of a rent book.

details of the landlord

Any tenant who occupies residential accommodation is entitled to be supplied with the name and address of his landlord by making a written request to his immediate landlord, the person who collects the rent or the landlord's agent. This information must be given within 21 days (not to do so is an offence with a fine of up to £500).

Where the landlord is a company, the tenant is entitled to have a list of the directors and the secretary.

A new landlord must give details of his name and address to the tenants within two months of the time he acquires the property. In practice, this generally happens more quickly, because he will have to produce an authority signed by the old landlord (or his agent) that the tenant should pay the rent to him.

sub-letting

A regulated tenant can sub-let unless the terms of his tenancy forbid it. But a statutory tenant who ceases to live in the premises loses the statutory tenancy, so he can only sub-let part.

If a tenant sub-lets on a regulated tenancy, he must give his landlord written notice of the sub-letting within 14 days and include details of the occupancy and rent.

controlled tenancies

This type of tenancy no longer exists. A controlled tenancy was one which was protected, before the coming into force of the Rent Act 1965, either under the Rent Acts 1920 to 1938 or under the Rent Act 1939. Its salient feature was that the rent was generally under £2 and could only be increased to take account of the cost of repairs and improvements, and then only by $12\frac{1}{2}$% of that cost. Many controlled tenancies became regulated tenancies by operation of the law prior to 1980, and section 64 of the Housing Act 1980 put paid to them finally. All controlled tenancies are now regulated tenancies within the fair rent system.

Now, in 1985, it is extremely unlikely that a tenant would be paying a controlled rent. Obviously it has been in landlords' best interests to apply for a fair rent to be registered immediately a controlled letting became a regulated one, this being the only way of obtaining a realistic rent from the tenant.

A controlled tenancy would have existed before 1980, where:

1 the tenant was living in the dwelling before 10 July 1957 or is the first successor of that tenant (if a second successor, the tenancy would have automatically become a regulated tenancy before 1980); *and*

2 the dwelling was unfurnished and owned by a private landlord; *and*

3 the rateable value of the dwelling on 31 March 1972 was less than

£70 in London or £35 elsewhere (if the rateable value was higher the tenancy became regulated by virtue of the Finance Act 1972); *and*

4 the rent was linked to the 1956 rateable value.

The Department of the Environment's booklet *Controlled Tenancies* explains how they were brought into the fair rent system.

Formerly controlled tenancies converted into regulated tenancies by the Housing Act 1980 or under the law prior to that date are otherwise subject to the normal law relating to regulated tenancies.

shorthold tenancies

The shorthold is a form of regulated tenancy introduced by the Housing Act 1980. It represents a move to encourage private landlords to let their property rather than sell it. They can create short lets of dwellings which will be free from the normal security of tenure provisions when the term expires, but still within the fair rent system. A shorthold can be created for a new tenancy only.

When first introduced, a condition to the grant of a shorthold was the compulsory registration of a fair rent. This is still true for lettings in Greater London but not for lettings elsewhere in England and Wales made on or after 1 December 1981.

Any dwelling that can be let on a normal protected tenancy can be let on shorthold. Basically this means that any non-resident private landlord can let furnished or unfurnished accommodation to a tenant on shorthold – provided that he fulfils certain conditions. The tenancy must be:

1 created after 28th November 1980;
  and

2 for a fixed term of between one and five years which cannot be brought to an end earlier by the landlord (unless the tenant breaks one of the terms of the agreement);
  and

3 to a new tenant: although it is impossible to convert the tenancy of an existing protected or statutory tenant into a shorthold, it is possible to offer that tenant a shorthold in some other accommodation, including another flat in the same building or different rooms in the same house. The tenant would be ill-advised

to accept such an offer because his security of tenure will be diminished;
and

4 prior to the grant of the tenancy, the landlord has given the tenant a notice in the form prescribed by statute;
and

5 for all shortholds granted before 1 December 1981 and all shortholds in Greater London whenever created, either

   (a) a fair rent has already been registered by the rent office, or

   (b) the landlord obtains a certificate of fair rent before the grant of the tenancy, and makes an application for the registration of a fair rent not later than 28 days after the start of the tenancy.

Compulsory rent registration is not a condition for shortholds granted on or after 1 December 1981 outside Greater London. If no fair rent is registered for the property, the landlord and tenant are free to agree any rent they choose. Such an agreement does not prejudice either party's right to apply to the rent officer to register a fair rent in the normal way.

the prescribed form of shorthold notice
There are different forms of notice for dwellings in Greater London and for dwellings elsewhere. The forms can be bought from law stationers. Both inform the tenant that he is being offered a shorthold tenancy. If the tenant is an existing protected or statutory tenant, he is warned that if he accepts a shorthold tenancy of other accommodation, including another flat in the same building, he will have less security of tenure.

The notice for Greater London details the registered rent, or records the fact that a certificate of fair rent has been obtained by the landlord and that he will be applying within 28 days of the start of the tenancy for the rent specified in the certificate to be registered. In either case, this is the highest rent a tenant can be charged until a higher rent is registered. Any excess paid by the tenant is recoverable (but only going back two years).

The notice for dwellings in England and Wales, not in Greater London, states the registered rent (if any) and says that this is the highest rent the tenant can be charged. If no fair rent has been registered for the accommodation, the agreed rent should be inserted. This is followed by a statement that either party may apply at any time to the rent officer for the registration of a fair rent.

the rights of the parties during the shorthold term

During the fixed term, the tenant is Rent Act protected. Unless the tenancy agreement provides for forfeiture for non-payment of rent or breach of any of the other terms of the tenancy, the landlord cannot bring the tenancy to a premature end.

The tenant, on the other hand, has the right to end the tenancy during the fixed term. If the term is for 2 years or less, he must give the landlord one month's notice in writing; if for over 2 years, three months' notice in writing. Any attempt to discourage the tenant from exercising this right by imposing on him any penalty or disability is void, and it is not possible to contract out of this right.

A shorthold tenant may not assign (that is transfer his interest in) the tenancy to someone else. He may, however, sub-let the whole or part of his accommodation – but only if the agreement permits him to do so. A sub-letting does not affect the landlord's right to regain possession at the end of the fixed term.

The court has power under the Matrimonial Homes Act 1983 to order the transfer of a shorthold tenancy from one spouse to the other, on granting a decree of divorce, nullity of marriage, or judicial separation, or at any time thereafter.

If the tenant dies during the shorthold term, the normal rules of succession under the Rent Act apply: the first successor takes a statutory tenancy which will end on the death of a second successor. Again, the right of the landlord to regain possession at the end of the shorthold term is unaffected.

the rights of the parties at the end of the fixed term

Case XIX, added to Schedule 15 of the Rent Act by the Housing Act 1980, gives the landlord a right to possession at the end of the shorthold term, provided he follows the correct procedure. This involves him in two separate stages. First, during the last three months of the shorthold term he must give the tenant at least three months' written notice of his intention to apply for a possession order under case XIX (known as 'the appropriate notice'). Second, he must take proceedings to obtain possession within three months of the expiry of the appropriate notice.

Provided that the landlord has fulfilled the conditions for creating a shorthold tenancy, has served a valid appropriate notice and taken proceedings within the proper time, the court must grant an order for possession against the tenant. If it thinks it just and equitable to do so, the court may grant the landlord a possession order even if he has not fulfilled certain of the shorthold conditions, namely serving the tenant with a shorthold notice before the tenant moved in, or complying with the compulsory rent registration requirement where applicable.

if time limits not observed

If the landlord fails to serve an appropriate notice of his intention to apply for possession under case XIX before the end of the fixed term, or fails to take proceedings within the three month time limit, he still retains the right to possession, but he must wait until three months before the anniversary of the end of the fixed term before he can serve his appropriate notice. So if, for example, the shorthold term ended on 31 December 1983, he may serve his appropriate notice at any time between 1 October and 31 December 1984, or 1 October and 31 December 1985, or 1 October and 31 December 1986 and so on. Proceedings must be taken within three months of the expiry of the appropriate notice.

The result, from the tenant's point of view, is that he can remain in possession on a yearly basis. Once the fixed term ends (or a successor becomes entitled to the tenancy) however, the tenant becomes a statutory tenant, and all the grounds for possession in Schedule 15 of the Rent Act become available to the landlord; he can offer suitable alternative accommodation, for instance. Furthermore, whatever the original shorthold agreement said, a statutory tenant cannot sub-let the whole of the premises. If he does, he loses the statutory tenancy.

Instead of just allowing a shorthold tenant or his successor to 'hold over' (that is, stay on) at the end of the shorthold term, the landlord may grant the tenant a new tenancy. This new tenancy cannot be a shorthold tenancy because it is granted to someone who was already a protected or statutory tenant. The new tenancy is an ordinary regulated tenancy, but the landlord still retains his right to recover possession under case XIX.

The housing booklet No 8 *Shorthold Tenancies* , a guide for private landlords and tenants, published by the Department of the Environment, includes specimen shorthold notices.

assured tenancies

To encourage the building of new housing for letting in the private sector, the Housing Act 1980 created an entirely new form of residential tenure called assured tenancies. Assured tenants fall outside the protection of the Rent Act 1977 and instead have security of tenure similar to that enjoyed by business tenants under the Landlord and Tenant Act 1954 Part II. This security is a statutory right to claim a renewal of the lease when it comes to an end, and compensation if a new lease is refused. The attraction of an assured tenancy from the landlord's point of view is that rents are fixed at an open market level.

Four conditions must be satisfied before an assured tenancy can be created. First, the landlord must be not an individual but a body approved by the Secretary of State. So far, several building societies, pension funds, property companies and building companies have been approved. Second, the premises must be newly built: construction work must have been started after 8 August 1980. At present, assured tenancies do not apply to conversions. The third condition is that before the tenant first occupied the property, no part of the premises had been lived in except on an assured tenancy. The last condition is that the tenancy would be a protected (or a housing association) tenancy were it not an assured tenancy. If these conditions are fulfilled, the tenant will be an assured tenant unless he is formally told to the contrary before the start of the tenancy.

rent
There is no control on the rent that can be charged at the beginning of an assured tenancy: it is for the parties to agree between themselves. And if an assured tenancy is renewed under the statutory procedure, the rent will be that payable on the open market.

security of tenure

An assured tenant cannot be evicted without a court order. This means that unless the tenant fails to pay rent or breaks some other term of the tenancy, he has security of tenure. When the original agreement expires, the assured tenancy continues automatically until either party starts the statutory procedure to end the tenancy.

A landlord who wants to end an assured tenancy at the end of the term and does not want to negotiate a new tenancy, must give at least six months' and not more than twelve months' notice in the prescribed form. If the tenant wishes to remain in his home, he must write to the landlord within 2 months, telling him so. He must also apply to the county court between 2 and 4 months of receiving the notice from the landlord.

A tenant who wishes to end the tenancy must give at least three months' notice in writing if his tenancy is for a fixed term; if periodic; an ordinary common law notice to quit of at least 4 weeks.

renewal

When the assured tenancy comes to an end, the parties no longer need to have regard to the statutory procedure and are free to negotiate and agree a new tenancy. If there is no agreement, the tenant has to serve the landlord with a notice in the prescribed form and apply to the county court for a new tenancy. The service of notices and taking of proceedings are governed by strict time limits and procedures and the tenant is advised to seek legal advice.

The landlord can oppose the grant of a new tenancy on one or more of the following grounds:

○ disrepair resulting from the tenant not having observed his repairing obligations under the current tenancy (only if the dwelling is in a very bad state of repair and the tenant does not remedy the situation before the date of the hearing)

○ persistent delay by the tenant in paying his rent

○ other substantial breaches by the tenant of the tenancy agreement

○ the landlord having offered the tenant suitable alternative accommodation (either an assured, protected [but not shorthold] or secure tenancy)

○ possession being required so that the whole of the dwelling can be let or disposed of as a single unit

○ the landlord intending to occupy the premises himself, or to demolish or reconstruct the property.

If the landlord cannot establish any of these grounds, the court may order that a new tenancy for up to fourteen years be granted, and has wide discretion as to the other terms of the tenancy.

compensation
If the landlord gains possession on the last two grounds above, or does not offer suitable alternative accommodation, he has to pay compensation to the tenant. The amount of compensation is $2\frac{1}{4}$ times the rateable value of the property. Any agreement purporting to exclude the tenant's right to compensation is invalid.

The Department of the Environment's booklet on *Assured Tenancies* provides a general guide for landlords and tenants about their rights and obligations and describes how landlords can become approved bodies to let homes on assured tenancies. It includes specimen forms.

tenancies for mixed residential and business purposes

Lettings of premises which are used for residential *and* business purposes are excluded from protection under the Rent Act 1977. Instead, they come under Part II of the Landlord and Tenant Act 1954 (which, like the Rent Act, applies only to tenancies, not licences). Although the Act defines 'business' widely to mean any trade, profession or employment, in the main its provisions affect small shops let with living accommodation above.

Sometimes premises are let for residential purposes and then used by the tenant for his business. Whether such activity constitutes the carrying on of a 'business', for the purposes of the Act, is a question of degree to be decided in the light of all the circumstances. If the tenant takes in lodgers, for example, the number of rooms, size of the establishment, sums involved and services provided, would all be relevant factors.

The protection is twofold: security of tenure and compensation for displacement. There is no initial rent control. In other words, the mixed residential and business tenant has much the same protection as the assured tenant.

security of tenure
The tenant cannot be evicted without a court order.

The tenancy continues until ended by the tenant serving notice to quit (for a periodic tenancy) or giving three months' notice (if his tenancy was for a fixed term), or the landlord can serve a notice in the prescribed form (available from law stationers) not less than 6 months or more than twelve months before the tenancy is to end. There are strict time limits and procedures for the serving of notices under the Act.

renewal
When the original tenancy comes to an end, the tenant has the right to ask for a new tenancy. This is done by using the prescribed form (on sale at law stationers). If the parties are not agreed as to the grant of a new tenancy, the tenant may apply to the court for one.

The court may grant a periodic or fixed tenancy for a period of up to fourteen years. The court has wide discretion to decide the other provisions of the new agreement. The terms of the new lease will be largely governed by the terms of the old lease, unless either party can show that a variation should be made in the light of accepted commercial practice which has changed since the old lease was granted. If the court has to fix a rent, this will be an open market rent, disregarding such factors as any goodwill attaching to the premises because of the tenant's business there and any improvements made by the tenant (other than any made because of a contractual obligation to the landlord).

The landlord can oppose the tenant's request for a new tenancy on any of the grounds set out in section 30 of the Act. These apply in the same way as for assured tenancies, except that an offer of suitable accommodation must take into account the tenant's business needs. Thus the landlord must offer and be willing to provide suitable alternative accommodation on terms which are reasonable, having regard to the terms of the current tenancy and to all other relevant circumstances. These will include: whether the goodwill attaching to the premises will be preserved, the nature and character of the tenant's business and the situation, size and other facilities of the premises under the current tenancy. If the court is satisfied that the landlord has offered suitable alternative accommodation, it cannot grant a new tenancy (that is, it will refuse the tenant's application).

The original tenancy continues until the court hearing, and any notice ending it does not take effect until three months after the final hearing.

compensation for displacement

If the landlord successfully opposes the grant of a new tenancy where the property is held on a sub-tenancy and the landlord wishes to let or sell it as a whole, or where he intends to reconstruct or demolish, or where he intends to occupy the premises for the purposes of his own business, compensation is payable when the tenant leaves. The amount is $3\frac{1}{4}$ times the rateable value of the premises. If for the past fourteen years the premises were occupied by the tenant or his predecessors in the same business, the compensation is doubled to six and a half times the rateable value.

The parties may agree to exclude the compensation for displacement provisions, but only where the tenant has occupied the premises for the purpose of his business for less than five years.

compensation for improvements

Very generally speaking, an outgoing tenant is entitled to compensation for improvements he has made to the premises, other than any he was obliged to make under the terms of his tenancy agreement.

sub-letting

A mixed residential and business tenant may sub-let the whole or part of his premises unless the agreement does not allow him to do so. Usually the agreement will state that the consent of the landlord must first be obtained. If so, it is implied that the landlord's consent shall not be unreasonably withheld.

restricted contracts

A tenancy which is not within the scope of the Rent Acts, may be within the definition of what is called a 'restricted contract', and so may a licence agreement. Restricted contracts are subject to a lesser degree of statutory interference than other forms of tenancy, with a system of rent control but no security of tenure. There are a number of restraints on the landlord attempting to regain possession, but these were greatly reduced by the Housing Act 1980 for contracts made after 28 November 1980.

A restricted contract may be in writing or oral.

The statutory definition of a restricted contract gives little clue to its actual identity – '*a contract . . . whereby one person grants to another person, in consideration of a rent which includes payment for the use of furniture or for services, the right to occupy a dwelling as a residence*'. In practice, a restricted contract will arise if there is:

(i) *A tenancy where there is a resident landlord.* The requirement as to furniture or services does not need to be satisfied if there is a resident landlord. A tenancy can fall within the restricted contract category even where the landlord is not resident provided he (or some other person) does share some essential living accommodation with the tenant – a kitchen or sitting room, for example (but sharing a bathroom or w.c. does not count).

Lettings by resident landlords comprise the largest group of agreements within the restricted sector.

(ii) *A tenancy or a licence where the rent includes payment for furniture or services.* 'Services' is defined to include attendance (cleaning and laundry), the provision of heating or lighting, the supply of

hot water and any other privilege or facility connected with the
occupancy of a dwelling, other than access, cold water supply or
w.c.

Most *tenancies* where furniture or services are provided are fully
protected under the Rent Act (regulated tenancies). The restricted
contract net will catch those which are excluded from full Rent Act
protection because, for instance, the rent includes a substantial
payment for attendance, or the tenancy is a student letting by an
educational establishment.

Exclusive occupation is implicit in tenancies that are restricted
contracts: a tenancy cannot exist without exclusive occupation.

For a *licence* to be a restricted contract, not only must furniture or
services be provided but the licensee must have exclusive occupation
of at least one room, usually the bedroom. An indication of what
this means can be found in the court's decision in a 1957 case. Mrs
F had a contract as a so-called 'paying guest' to occupy an upper
room in the P household. Lord Goddard said *"The test is: had Mrs
F the exclusive right to use the room as a residence? Mrs P, having let
this room as a residence to Mrs F, had no right to come in and occupy
it herself, nor had she a right to put somebody else into the room. I
think that Mrs F had the exclusive right to use the room as a residence."*

In later cases, restricted contracts have been found to exist in
connection with a hotel room, a room in a YMCA hostel and
accommodation in a self-catering hotel for single men, but it has
been stressed that the accommodation must be more than of a
temporary nature. Usually service licences are not restricted
contracts because rent is not paid.

In the following discussion, the word 'tenant' is used to describe the
occupier under a restricted contract, be he tenant or licensee.

not a restricted contract
The basic definition of a restricted contract is qualified by excluding
certain types of agreement. The agreement will not be a restricted
contract where:

○ the rateable value of the occupier's part of the premises is more
than £1,500 in Greater London and £750 elsewhere;

○ the rent includes a substantial payment for board (that is meals);

○ the landlord is the Crown, a government department or local authority, a registered housing association, housing trust, the Housing Corporation or a housing cooperative;

○ the letting is a regulated tenancy with full Rent Act protection;

○ the contract is to occupy a dwelling for a holiday.

It is essential for the occupier to have some accommodation which excludes other residential occupiers. The fact that he shares other accommodation does not matter. One sure way, therefore, in which a landlord may avoid the statutory provision relating to both regulated tenancies and restricted contracts is to deny the occupier exclusive possession. This would be done by inserting in the agreement a clause to the effect that the landlord or some other person has a right to live in the accommodation. Another way is to provide proper meals, or to create a holiday let. In these cases, the occupier can rely only on his limited contractual rights under the agreement.

rent control
If there is no registered rent for the premises, the rent is entirely a matter for agreement between the parties. But either the landlord or the tenant, or both of them together, or the local authority, may apply to the rent tribunal for a reasonable rent to be determined and registered. The rent tribunal is the rent assessment committee in another guise. Its composition is the same, namely a layman, a surveyor and a lawyer-chairman.

An application to the rent tribunal is made on a standard prescribed form, FR2, available from the clerk to the tribunal. The names and addresses of the landlord and tenant must be given together with the address of the premises, details of the accommodation and any furniture and services provided, the rent payable and any meals supplied. A copy of any written agreement should accompany the form.

Provided that an application has not been withdrawn 'before the tribunal have entered upon consideration of it' (which apparently means before all the panel members have started to read the papers), they must consider it, make the appropriate enquiries (which often includes a visit to the premises) and either arrange a hearing or ask for written representations from the parties. If a hearing is called, it is fairly informal and will follow much the same format as a hearing before the rent assessment committee. To help it make a decision, the rent tribunal may ask the landlord to furnish it with certain information. Wilful refusal on the part of a landlord so to do is a criminal offence.

If there is any doubt whether there is a restricted contract, a resolution of the court under section 141 of the Rent Act will have to be sought.

'reasonable rent'

The reasonable rent which the tribunal arrives at may be higher, or lower, or the same as the existing one. Unlike the assessment of a fair rent, there is no statutory provision about factors the tribunal much take into account (age, state and condition of the premises and so on) or disregard (scarcity value, for example). Reasonable rents may therefore be higher than fair rents but lower than market rents. The tribunal notifies its decision to the parties in writing but is not bound to give reasons for it, unless specifically asked to do so. There is no appeal from a tribunal decision except to the High Court on a point of law or matter of natural justice.

All reasonable rents are entered on a register maintained by the tribunal. This is open to public inspection, so anyone who is intending to let or rent accommodation under a restricted contract can see what a reasonable rent is likely to be.

Where a reasonable rent is registered, this is the maximum rent the landlord can charge until it is cancelled (so it continues to apply to a new tenant). He commits a criminal offence if he charges more. Any excess rent the tenant has paid is recoverable from the landlord. If necessary, the tenant has to take county court proceedings to get back the overpayment.

If the registered rent is higher than the previous one, the tenant must pay it immediately. The increase is not subject to phasing.

A reasonable rent does not include rates. If the landlord pays rates for the accommodation, he can recover these (and any increase in rates) from the tenant, in addition to the reasonable rent.

cancellation

An application for the cancellation of a registered rent may be made to the rent tribunal if the following conditions are satisfied:

(i) the registration is at least 2 years old; *and*

(ii) the accommodation is not currently subject to a restricted contract (for example because it is empty); *and*

(iii) the application is made by the person who would, but for (ii), be the landlord.

The application for cancellation must be made on a special form, obtainable from the clerk to the tribunal. The cancellation of a registered rent does not prejudice any future application for the registration of a reasonable rent, if there is a new letting.

In addition, either the landlord, or the tenant or the local authority may apply to the tribunal to review or reconsider the rent, provided that two years or more have elapsed since the date they considered it last. Such an application may then be made at any time where

○ the landlord and tenant apply jointly; or

○ there is a change in the condition of the accommodation, the furniture or services supplied, the terms of the contract or any other circumstances accounted for in the tribunal's previous decision.

Application has to be made on a standard form.

no premiums

If a reasonable rent is registered for the premises (but not otherwise) it is illegal to charge a premium for the grant or assignment of a restricted contract. The landlord may take a deposit from the tenant against non-payment of bills or damage to furniture and so on, but this must not be more than two months' rent.

rent books

Where rent is payable weekly under a restricted contract, the landlord has to provide a rent book, containing certain notices and particulars of rent and of the other terms and conditions of the contract.

terminating a restricted contract

If the tenant entered into a restricted contract after 28 November 1980, he has no security of tenure. If he has a *periodic tenancy*, the landlord must give at least four weeks' notice in the prescribed form. In the case of a *fixed term tenancy*, no notice to quit is normally required: the tenancy will come to an end when the fixed term expires. The same is true of a licence. However, where the terms of the agreement provide for a notice to quit to be given, the landlord will have to comply.

Irrespective of whether the contract amounts to a tenancy or a licence, there can be no eviction without a court order for possession. When the notice to quit expires, or at the end of the fixed term or licence, the landlord must go to the court if the tenant or licensee does not leave. Proceedings are taken in the county court and, although possession cannot be refused, the court has the power to postpone the date on which it must be given. The postponement cannot be for longer than 3 months. When possession is postponed, the court will impose conditions on the tenant regarding the payment of current rent and any arrears (unless exceptional hardship would be caused to the tenant, or it is otherwise unreasonable). If the tenant breaks these conditions or otherwise misbehaves (uses the accommodation for immoral purposes, for instance) the landlord may ask the court for an earlier date for possession. But to prevent an unlawful eviction, the landlord needs to obtain a warrant for possession.

pre-November 1980 restricted contracts
If the contract was entered into before 28 November 1980, the tenant still has no security of tenure but is in a better position because of the greater delaying devices available to him. With pre-1980 contracts, a distinction has to be drawn between contracts which are determinable by notice to quit and those which are not.

The following rules apply only where a valid notice to quit has been served (for periodic tenancies, this is at least 4 weeks notice in the prescribed form; for fixed term tenancies and licences which require notices to quit, it has to be a notice which complies with the terms of the agreement and allows a reasonable time for the quitting of the premises).

(i) If a notice to quit is served *by the landlord* after the tenant has applied to the rent tribunal for a reasonable rent to be assessed, the notice is automatically suspended until six months after the rent tribunal's decision. (This period can be reduced by the tribunal.) When the period has expired, the tenant may apply for a further postponement under a different section (see ii below) of the Act. There is no limit to the number of postponements that can be applied for.

(ii) Where a notice to quit has been served by *either party* and the contract has been referred to the rent tribunal for the determination of a reasonable rent (before or after the notice to quit has been served), the tenant may apply to the tribunal for a postponement of the notice. But he must do so before the notice expires. The notice is then postponed until the tribunal reaches its decision as to the rent, and the tribunal may, as part of its decision, suspend the operation of the notice for up to six months from the date on which it would otherwise have expired – that is, for example, at the end of an extension under (i) above, or a previous postponement under this (ii) paragraph. The tribunal is not bound to exercise this discretion and, if it refuses to do so, the notice is postponed for 7 days after the tribunal's decision and the tenant cannot apply for a further extension.

If the tenant breaks the terms of the contract or otherwise misbehaves (causes a nuisance to neighbours, for instance) during any period of suspension, the landlord can go back to the tribunal and ask them to bring forward the date for possession.

These rules depend on a valid notice to quit having been served, so they apply in the main to periodic tenancies only. Fixed term tenants and licensees (whose agreements provide that occupation shall cease on a certain date) have no right to remain when their term ends.

If a landlord granted a fixed-term tenancy to an existing tenant, before 28 November 1980 (that is, a second tenancy which was for a fixed term), the tenant will be a fully protected tenant under the Rent Act and therefore entitled to remain in possession after the end of the fixed term.

The Department of the Environment's booklet *Letting Rooms in Your House* (a guide for resident landlords and their tenants) includes a section on the special rules which apply to lettings that began before 28 November 1980.

special note for resident landlords

If a landlord ceases to be a resident landlord on a permanent basis, the restricted contract tenancy becomes a regulated tenancy under the Rent Act. However, in the following two situations the letting will remain a restricted contract even where the landlord is not resident:

○ If the premises are sold and the buyer (the new landlord) gives the tenant notice within 28 days that he intends to take up residence and does so within six months.

○ If a resident landlord has died, two years are allowed for the winding-up of the estate. During this period, a person who has inherited the dwelling may move into residence, or the personal representatives of the deceased landlord may exercise the rights of a resident landlord to obtain possession. If the property is owned by joint tenants and the survivor does not live at the property (although for this exception to operate at all, one of the joint owners must have lived there) it will be that person, the survivor, who is entitled to obtain vacant possession of the property, by serving the appropriate notice and obtaining the court order for possession.

long tenancies at low rents

The Rent Act 1977 does not cover residential tenants with a long lease at a low rent. The basic protection given to residential occupiers by the Protection from Eviction Act applies, however, and the Landlord and Tenant Act 1954 and the Leasehold Reform Act 1967 give them valuable rights, both during and at the end of the tenancy.

the Landlord and Tenant Act 1954

If a tenant has a long lease *and* he pays a low rent, he will be unprotected unless he comes within Part I of the Landlord and Tenant Act 1954.

A long lease is one which is granted for a term of over 21 years and which cannot be ended prematurely by a landlord's notice. A low rent is one that is less than $\frac{2}{3}$ of the rateable value of the property. Sums payable for maintenance, services, insurance and rates are disregarded from the calculation, and the appropriate rateable value for this purpose is the rateable value on 23 March 1965 or when first rated, if later. The tenancy must be one which, apart from its low rent, would otherwise be within the Rent Act. Basically, there must be a letting of accommodation which the tenant occupies as his home, within certain rateable value limits.

security of tenure

During the fixed term, the landlord can regain possession only if the tenant breaks the terms of his tenancy agreement and then only by going through the courts. When the fixed term runs out, the tenancy continues on the same terms until ended by the landlord or the tenant in the proper manner.

A tenant can terminate the tenancy by giving one month's notice. He can serve this early, so that the notice expires on the original term date. A landlord must serve not less than 6 months' nor more than 12 months' notice on the tenant. His notice must include either .

○ proposals for a new statutory tenancy specifying the accommodation, the rent and other terms of the agreement; or

○ a warning that if the tenant is not willing to give up possession, the landlord will apply to the court for possession on stated grounds.

The parties should agree to the terms of the statutory tenancy or apply to the court to settle the matter within two months, otherwise the notice lapses. When the terms have been decided, the tenant has an ordinary statutory tenancy under the Rent Act 1977. All the grounds for possession apply and either party may ask for the registration of a fair rent.

Alternatively, if the landlord wants possession, grounds on which he can seek possession are

○ that the tenant has not paid the rent, or has broken some other term of the tenancy

○ that the tenant or a person living with him has caused a nuisance or annoyance to neighbours or has been convicted of immoral or illegal use of the premises

○ that the landlord requires the property for his family or himself

○ that the landlord has offered suitable alternative accommodation.

These grounds are discretionary: the court may grant an order for possession if it thinks it reasonable to do so. If the order is refused, the tenancy continues on the same terms are before.

the Leasehold Reform Act 1967

The Leasehold Reform Act 1967 gives valuable rights to tenants in the private and public sector who are occupying a house under a long lease at a low rent (commonly called a ground rent). The leases were often 'building' leases at a very low ground rent for terms of 99 or 125 years. The tenant therefore built and maintained a house which at the end of the term became the landlord's entitlement. The problem became great in the 1960's when many such leases expired. The purpose of the Act is to allow the tenant

○ to buy the freehold (the tenant's right to enfranchise); or

○ to extend the period of the lease for up to 50 years; or

○ to remain in occupation of the property when the lease expires, as a statutory tenant.

A tenant who wishes to buy the freehold or extend the lease must give the landlord notice of this intention before the original term granted by the lease expires.

The tenant must meet all the following conditions:

 i he must have a lease of a house; *and*

 ii the lease must be for a long term; *and*

 iii the rent must be a low rent; *and*

 iv the rateable value of the house must fall within prescribed limits; *and*

 v he must have occupied the house as his only or main residence for the whole of the last three years, or for a total of three out of the last ten years.

a house
Most detached, semi-detached and terraced houses satisfy the 'house' condition. The Act does not contain an exhaustive definition of the word, but lays down certain broad rules:

○ The fact that a building is not structurally detached does not prevent it from being a house.

○ An individual maisonette or flat cannot be a house, but the whole building may be even though it is divided horizontally into maisonettes or flats. So, if a tenant of a large house divides it into flats, lets the upper floors and lives in the ground floor flat himself, he will be able to buy the freehold or extend his lease of the house, but his tenants cannot.

○ If the building is divided vertically into units, it is not a house, but the individual units may be.

Problems may arise when accommodation is used for mixed residential and business purposes and cannot be divided into separate vertical units. The House of Lords have held that as long as such accommodation can reasonably be called a house, it will come under the Act, provided it satisfies the other conditions.

a long lease
A long lease is one which has been granted for a term of more than twenty-one years. The tenant does not have to be the original tenant, he may be an assignee (that is, someone who has bought the lease).

Where the tenant's term of the lease was originally for less than 21 years but has been renewed, he may have a long lease if the original and renewed terms together add up to more than 21 years. No premium (lump sum) must have been paid for the renewal.

Landlords used to be able to avoid the Act by granting a lease terminable by notice after any death or marriage. This loophole was narrowed by the Housing Act 1980 for leases granted after 18 April 1980. Now such a provision can help the landlord only if

○ the notice can only be served within three months after the tenant's death or marriage (nobody else's)

and

○ the lease contains an absolute prohibition on selling or sub-letting the whole of the property.

a low rent
The annual rent must be less than two-thirds of the rateable value of the house assessed on 23 March 1965, or the date on which the property first appeared in the valuation list, or the first day of the

term granted by the lease, whichever is the later. The local authority's valuation officer will help with enquiries relating to rateable values.

A lease will be outside the Act if it was granted between 31 August 1939 and 1 April 1963 and the rent at the beginning of the tenancy was more than two-thirds of the letting value of the property. The 'letting value' of a property is the amount which could be obtained by a landlord letting on the open market.

Any amounts paid by a tenant towards the landlord's costs of insuring the building, providing services or carrying out repairs are to be disregarded in calculating 'low rents', irrespective of when the lease was created.

rateable values
The relevant date, known as 'the appropriate day', on which the rateable value is taken is 23 March 1965, or if later, the date when the property first appeared in the valuation list for rating purposes.

Here is a table of the limits, if the tenancy was granted:

	on or before *18 February 1966*	*on or after* *19 February 1966*
Greater London	(a) £400; or (b) £1,500 if the	(a) £400; or (b) £1,000 if the
	property appears in the valuation list for the first time after 1 April 1973	
Elsewhere	(a) £200; or (b) £750 if the	(a) £200; or (b) £500 if the
	property appears in the valuation list for the first time after 1 April 1973	

Note
If the 'appropriate date' was before 1 April 1973 and the rateable value was more than £400 (in Greater London) or £200 (elsewhere), then 1 April 1973 is substituted as 'the appropriate day' and provided the rateable value is not more than £1500 (in Greater London) or £750 (elsewhere), the property will be within the prescribed limits. This provision does not apply to tenancies granted on or after 19 February 1966.

The rateable value of some properties was re-assessed to take effect from 1 April 1973. If the rateable value was increased because of improvements made by the tenant or his predecessors, the tenant may be entitled to a notional reduction for the purpose of bringing the house within the rateable value limits (but not for assessing rates payable). A tenant who is entitled to a notional reduction should inform his landlord in writing (there is a prescribed form for this, which requires details of the improvements and who paid for them) and ask the landlord to agree a figure for the reduction, within six weeks. If no agreement is reached, the tenant may apply (between six and twelve weeks after service of the notice) to the county court for it to decide the reduction. The court office will inform the tenant how to make an application.

three years' occupation

If a tenant occupies a house for two years by virtue of a monthly tenancy and then takes a long lease of the house at a low rent, the first two years of occupation cannot be used to fulfil the three-year condition: he must wait until three years have elapsed from the date he took the long lease.

If the tenant inherited the lease, any period of occupation by a member of his family who was the previous tenant can count towards the three year period, provided the tenant was during that time also living in the house. 'Member of the family' includes husband or wife, son, daughter (including adopted children, step-children and illegitimate children), son-in-law or daughter-in-law of the tenant or of the tenant's wife or husband, and the father or mother of the tenant or tenant's wife or husband.

The tenant need not live in the whole of the house. He still comes within the Act if he lets off part, provided he has occupied that or some other part as his only or main residence for the whole of the last three years or a total of three years during the last ten.

the right to buy the freehold

A tenant has the right to buy only that which was the subject matter of a lease covered by the Act. He cannot compel the landlord to sell him a garden, garage or outbuilding which he has been using unless it was also included in the lease of the house, nor has he a right to buy a garage or garden let to him under a totally different lease. It is perfectly permissible, however, for the tenant to agree to buy these separately from a landlord. (They will probably be of little use to the landlord or anyone else.)

A landlord may suffer hardship if he is forced to sell his house to a tenant, while himself retaining another part of the same building. For example, the landlord may have the use of one small room in a building, the rest of which is the tenant's house. To sell the house to the tenant may well render that small room valueless. Where this is the case, the landlord may, within two months of receiving notice that his tenant wishes to enfranchise, serve a notice on the tenant objecting to the severance of the house from the rest of the building (in our example, the small room) and asking the tenant to agree to buy it along with the house. If the tenant does not object, a price for the remainder of the building has to be agreed. The landlord can ask any price he wants for that small room. If agreement cannot be reached, the matter will ultimately have to be referred to the county court to decide whether it is reasonable for the tenant to buy the part of the building specified in the landlord's notice.

A similar procedure exists when a landlord wishes to reduce the extent of the premises he is statutorily bound to sell to his tenant. Again, if the landlord and tenant cannot agree about the reduction, the matter can be referred to the county court. In deciding, the court will have regard to any hardship which would be caused to the tenant if it grants the reduction of the premises (and vice versa).

Legal ownership of a house does not merely mean owning bricks and mortar. It includes a bundle of legal rights necessary for the proper enjoyment of the house, for example to use pipes and cables crossing a neighbour's land for the supply of electricity, water and other services, and to use a private road running along the back of the house. A tenant will normally be expressly granted such rights in his lease.

The Act ensures that when the tenant buys the freehold, he will enjoy similar rights. In so far as the landlord is able, he must grant to his buyer-tenant such rights as are necessary to ensure that the buyer's position is the same as when he was a tenant.

The Act also ensures that the landlord and neighbours retain any rights that they enjoyed before the tenant enfranchised. When the landlord sells the freehold interest in the house, he may insist on retaining some of the rights which he (or some other person) enjoyed over part of the buyer-tenant's house when it was held under the long lease.

the price

The policy behind the Leasehold Reform Act is to treat the tenant as the owner of the building and the landlord merely as the owner of the land on which the house stands. The tenant is, accordingly, able to buy the freehold at a favourable price.

The price payable will be the open market value of the freehold in the house subject to one of two sets of assumptions laid down by the Act, based on the rateable value of the house on the date the tenant gives the landlord notice of his intention to buy the freehold.

If the rateable value is £1,000 or less in Greater London, or £500 or less elsewhere, the assumptions are that

○ the landlord is selling the freehold subject to the tenancy and the tenancy has been extended under the Act

○ the landlord is willing to sell but the tenant does not have the right to compel him to sell

○ the sale is subject to and with the benefits of the existing rights, and subject to the existing incumbrances affecting the property (provided that these will bind the tenant once the sale is completed)

○ any defect in the title of the landlord would result in a discount in accordance with the principle applicable to sales on the open market

○ the tenant does not have any special interest in buying the landlord's reversionary interest.

If the rateable value in Greater London is between £1,001 and £1,500, and elsewhere is between £501 and £750, the assumptions are that

○ the landlord is selling the freehold subject to the tenancy

○ at the end of the tenancy, the tenant will have the right to remain in occupation under the provisions of Part I of the Landlord and Tenant Act 1954

○ the tenant has no liability to carry out repairs either under the terms of the lease or the provisions of Part I of the Landlord and Tenant Act 1954

○ the value of the house has not been increased by any improvements made by the tenant

○ the sale is subject to and with the benefit of the rights and subject to existing incumbrances affecting the enjoyment of the property (provided that these will bind the tenant once the sale is completed).

The principal difference between the two bases is that in the first (where the rateable value is lower) the increased value of the landlord's reversion (the freehold) to the tenant is ignored as if a third party were buying. If the property were sold to a third party, it would be sold subject to the long lease without vacant possession and the price would have to be discounted to take account of this fact. If, however, the tenant, rather than a third party, buys the freehold, his leasehold interest disappears and he then has a freehold which is not subject to any sort of lease. In other words, the freehold is much more valuable to the tenant than to a third party buyer.

disputes as to the price
A landlord or a tenant may ask the local leasehold valuation tribunal (the address is the same as for the rent assessment committee and can be found in the telephone directory) to determine the price to be paid by a tenant who wishes to buy the freehold under the Act. A tenant may apply as soon as the landlord has named a price or after two months from the date he served his notice of intention to buy. Application is made on form 1, obtainable from the law stationers or the tribunal's offices.

The leasehold valuation tribunal is made up of three people drawn from the rent assessment panel for the area. One member must be a qualified valuer. There is no fee for applying to the tribunal.

A hearing date is set by the tribunal. At the hearing, both parties are given the opportunity to state their case, calling such witnesses as they feel necessary. The proceedings tend to be informal. Shortly after the hearing, each party to the application is sent a document by the tribunal, stating the price (and such other decisions as may be relevant) and the reasons for their decision.

Either party may appeal to the lands tribunal against a decision by the leasehold valuation tribunal. Appeal must be made within 28 days of the latter's decision. A fee is payable and the unsuccessful party may have to pay or contribute towards the other's costs.

covenants, when a tenant enfranchises

A lease contains a variety of covenants, promises on the part of both landlord and tenant dealing, amongst other things, with the payment of rent, insurance, repair, use of the property and so on. Most of these covenants obviously become inappropriate when the tenant buys the freehold, and so they disappear.

The landlord can, however, retain a certain degree of control over the buyer-tenant's future use and enjoyment of the property. He has the right to sell the freehold subject to any restrictive covenants in the long lease which benefit any other property he owns. Suppose the lease contains a provision that the tenant 'shall not use the property as a public house or inn'. As long as the landlord can prove that he owns other property which will benefit from this covenant, he can insist that the freehold is sold to the tenant subject to a similar provision.

'scheme of arrangement'
A tenant who lives on an estate controlled by a single landlord may have to buy the freehold subject to a 'scheme of arrangement'. Such landlords often use covenants in leases to their tenants to control the general appearance of the estate. If the tenants enfranchise, these

covenants would disappear and possibly lead to a deterioration in the appearance of the estate. The landlord can apply to the High Court to have a scheme of arrangement approved, so that he will retain the power to

○ carry out work for the maintenance or repair of any property which was formerly leasehold but which has been bought by a tenant;

○ regulate development of, and impose restrictions on, the use of such properties;

○ require a tenant who has bought the freehold under the Act to contribute towards the maintenance and repair of the property where the (ex-)landlord has incurred expense for this purpose under the scheme.

A tenant should be able to find out from his landlord if there is an approved scheme. Failing this, a search of the register of local land charges will reveal its existence or non-existence. A local land charges search is made with the local district council (or in London the appropriate borough council) on form LLCI. The cost of the search is £2.65. It takes approximately three weeks to receive the reply to a search.

The local authority may also be able to provide a tenant with a copy of the scheme so that the full extent of the 'landlord's' powers can be appreciated. It would be prudent for a purchaser, as well as making a search in the local land charges register, to submit a form of enquiries of the local authority which will reveal information as to roads, drainage and many other matters which a freehold owner of property ought to know. If the forms are all submitted together, the cost is £12.30.

mortgages

A landlord may have mortgaged his interest in the property – perhaps to enable him to buy it in the first place. What happens to such a mortgage if the tenant acquires the freehold?

When a freehold interest is conveyed or transferred to the tenant, the tenant's house is released from the mortgage but he must pay the purchase price to the landlord's mortgagee (the lender) in discharge of the mortgage. (If there is more than one mortgage to be paid off, they must be paid off in order of priority, broadly speaking according to the date on which they were created. In cases of doubt, a solicitor should be consulted.)

It is extremely important for a tenant first to find out if his landlord (or anyone else with a superior interest) has a mortgage, and to ensure that the purchase price is paid to that mortgagee. If the tenant does not pay the purchase price to his landlord's mortgagee, the property he buys will remain subject to the mortgage to the extent of the purchase price.

It is not necessary for the landlord to obtain the mortgagee's consent to the sale, nor for a mortgagee to be joined as a party to the conveyance or transfer.

If the tenant cannot discover whether the landlord has mortgaged his interest, or the identity of a mortgagee, he should pay the purchase price into court. The same is true if a mortgagee proves to be unhelpful and, for example, refuses to sign a release of the house from the mortgage. The county court office will tell the tenant how to do this.

The fact that the house and premises are released from the mortgage does not necessarily mean that the mortgage will be completely paid off. If the purchase price is not sufficient to pay off the total amount of the landlord's indebtedness to the mortgagee, the landlord will still remain liable to pay off the balance.

In certain cases, where on 27 October 1967 the landlord's estate was subject to both a mortgage and a long tenancy with not more than twenty years to run, the landlord may apply to the court to have his obligations under the mortgage modified or discharged altogether. Again, the county court office will inform a landlord of the procedure for claiming this relief.

the right to extend the lease

The tenant who cannot afford to buy the freehold or does not wish to do so, may choose to claim an extension of his existing lease. Once a tenant gives notice to his landlord that he wishes to claim an extension, the landlord has to grant him a new tenancy in substitution for the existing one.

The terms of that new lease will be as follows:

1 *Duration:* The landlord has to grant an extension of fifty years. The new lease will expire 50 years after the date on which, but for the Act, the existing lease would have expired.

2 *Property included in the new lease:* Broadly speaking, the premises comprised in the new lease will be the same as those contained in the tenant's existing lease. However, similar to the situation when a tenant exercises his right to buy the freehold, the landlord may increase or reduce the premises to be included in the new lease.

3 *Rent:* The tenant continues to pay the agreed rent until the date on which his existing lease expires. Thereafter, he has to pay a new 'ground rent', based on the letting value of the land on which the house stands (ignoring any value attributable to the house or other buildings). The use to which the land may be put will be taken into consideration. Thus if the site is ripe for redevelopment, the rent will reflect this and be higher.

The landlord can require the new ground rent to be reviewed after twenty-five years; he has to serve notice on the tenant during the twenty-fourth year of the new lease. The reviewed ground rent is calculated in the same way as the new ground rent was.

Any payment towards services which the landlord has to provide under the terms of the new tenancy will be in addition to the new ground rent. If the tenant's existing lease requires him to contribute a fixed sum towards services and over the course of time this figure has become unrealistic, the Act says that 'such provision as may be just' should be made for payments by the tenant. Failing agreement between the parties, the leasehold valuation tribunal may be asked to fix a figure.

The leasehold valuation tribunal has the power to fix a new ground rent, on the application of either the landlord or the tenant. Application is made on form 2 (*Application for determination by leasehold valuation tribunal of the rent to be payable*), which contains 13 questions most of which are self explanatory.

The amount of the new ground rent (and any reviewed rent) must not be assessed until the year before the tenant's existing lease is to expire (or the twenty-fourth year of the extended period). This is to ensure that in a fluctuating property market a fair rent is arrived at.

4 *Other terms:* As a general rule, the provisions of the new lease will be the same as those in the tenant's existing lease. There are some important exceptions to this:

(i) Where the property to be included in the new lease is not exactly the same as that in the original one, the new lease may contain any necessary modifications. For instance, if the landlord has reduced the premises originally let to the tenant, his repair obligations under the new lease will be less extensive.

(ii) A right to renew, or a right of pre-emption (that is a right of first refusal) in respect of the reversion, or an option to buy the reversion will be excluded from the new lease. A tenant should think carefully whether he wishes to lose these valuable rights.

(iii) The new lease will not contain a provision which allows the landlord to terminate the tenancy prematurely, otherwise than in the event of breach of covenant by the tenant.

(iv) The new lease must contain a provision that no long sub-tenancy can confer on the sub-tenant any right to buy the freehold or extend the sub-tenancy under the Act.

(v) The new lease must provide that the landlord has the right to resume possession of the property for the purposes of redeveloping it. Section 17 gives the landlord the right to seek possession from the court at any time, if he can prove that for the purposes of redevelopment he proposes to demolish or reconstruct the whole or a substantial part of the property.

A landlord who successfully obtains possession against a tenant under Section 17 will have to pay compensation. The amount of compensation is what the house would be expected to realise in the open market if sold by a willing seller on certain assumptions – such as that the property is vacant and subject to existing incumbrances and restrictions and not subject to a tenant's right to buy the freehold.

If the parties cannot agree a figure for compensation, either can apply to the leasehold valuation tribunal for the matter to be settled. Application is made on Form 3 (*Application for determination by leasehold valuation tribunal of compensation payable to a tenant*).

tenant loses right to buy the freehold
When a tenant claims an extension under the Act he retains his right to buy the freehold, but only until the date on which his original lease expires. So, if he does not serve the landlord with notice of his intention to buy the freehold before that date, he will have to give up possession at the end of his extended 50 years lease. He has no right to a further extension under the Act and is not protected by the Rent Act.

A tenant should remember that his lease will almost certainly contain a covenant by him to repair the property. At the end of his lease he will be required to ensure that the property is in a good state of repair. The landlord may serve a schedule of dilapidations setting out the work he feels necessary to put the premises in proper order. If a tenant has failed to meet his repair obligations during the tenancy, he may have to pay for the repairs in one lump sum.

the tenant's right to stay on

A tenant may choose not to exercise his right to buy the freehold or claim an extended lease, or perhaps he will not have occupied the property for the qualifying period of three years before the long lease expires. In these circumstances, provided that the property is within the current rateable value limits laid down by the Rent Act, the tenant has the right to remain in possession of the property as a statutory tenant.

Briefly, a statutory tenant has the right to remain in possession and on his death a member of his family may succeed to the statutory tenancy. A statutory tenant may apply to have a fair rent registered for the property.

opposing a tenant's claim to enfranchise or to an extended lease

If the conditions laid down by the Act are not satisfied, the tenant cannot claim any of the rights conferred by it.

A landlord may oppose a claim by his tenant to buy the freehold or extend the lease on one of several grounds.

1 landlord requires the property for his own occupation

The landlord may apply to the county court for possession of the house when the original lease expires. He must apply during the term of the original lease but after the tenant has served notice claiming his rights under the Act. The court office will help with applications.

To oppose the tenant's claim successfully the landlord must show

○ that he acquired his interest in the house before 19 February 1966

○ that the house or part of it is, or will be, reasonably required by him, or an adult (over 18) member of his family, as his or their only or main residence on the date the tenant's original lease expires. For this purpose, member of a landlord's family includes spouse, son or daughter, son- or daughter-in-law, father or mother, father- or mother-in-law; adopted, illegitimate and step-children qualify.

○ that it would cause greater hardship to him or the member of the family if the court did not make an order for possession than would be the case if the tenant had to give up possession at the end of the lease. The landlord must produce sufficient evidence of the hardship.

The court has absolute discretion as to the granting of such orders. If the landlord is successful, the court will make an order specifying a date when he can re-take possession. The tenant will be entitled to compensation for his loss of the house and premises, the amount of which is assessed as if a landlord re-takes possession for the purposes of redevelopment.

A landlord who makes an unsuccessful application to the court on this ground may submit another application if his circumstances change.

2   redevelopment

A landlord whose tenant has claimed an extended lease may regain possession if he intends to demolish or reconstruct the whole or a substantial part of the premises for the purposes of redevelopment. Compensation is payable to the outgoing tenant.

The Act contains special provisions applicable to landlords which are public authorities such as county and district councils, universities, nationalised industries, health authorities and so on. If a public authority obtains a certificate from the appropriate minister (usually the Secretary for State for the Environment) stating that it will need the property for development within the next ten years, that public authority will be able to resist a tenant's claim to buy the freehold or extend the lease. Again, a tenant whose rights under the Act are taken away in this manner is entitled to compensation.

3   where the Crown has an interest

Generally speaking, the Crown is not bound by the provisions of the Act and the tenant may find that he is unable to take advantage of the Act.

In practice, however, the Crown usually allows a tenant to exercise his right to enfranchise or extend his lease, unless the property is of special architectural or historic interest or is needed for development or some public purposes.

If the Crown is not the tenant's immediate landlord and the tenant is only claiming an extended lease, provided that the immediate landlord has at least fifty years' leasehold interest in the property, the tenant can proceed in the normal way and the Crown's interest can then generally be ignored.

4   tenant has previously given a notice to quit

If the landlord can prove that a tenant's notice claiming to acquire the freehold or an extended lease is made after a tenant has given notice to quit, the claim is invalid.

The Act provides that if a tenant makes a claim under the Act towards the end of his original lease, the tenancy is not to expire and cannot be terminated by a landlord serving notice to quit. The lease is extended for so long as the claim by the tenant is being dealt with, plus a further three months of grace afterwards.

special provisions relating to sub-tenants

The fact that the tenant in occupation is a sub-tenant (or a
sub-sub-tenant) does not prevent him from buying the freehold,
claiming an extended lease, or staying on as a statutory tenant,
provided all the conditions for the application of the Act are
otherwise fulfilled. The Act makes special provision to enable all the
superior interests (that is the interest of the tenant in occupation's
landlord and other interests higher up the chain) to be dealt with.

the reversioner
To simplify the procedure, the Act states that the tenant shall deal
with one person only – 'the reversioner'. He has the power to
conduct the proceedings, once a sub-tenant has given notice claiming
his statutory rights. He can execute a conveyance of the freehold to
the sub-tenant or grant a new extended lease, and he binds any
landlords with interests superior to the tenant in occupation.
Furthermore, the reversioner is entitled to call upon all landlords
with superior interests to produce documents in order to ensure that
the tenant gets good title.

The reversioner may be:

(a) the first landlord higher up the chain of tenancies from the tenant
in occupation who (on expiry of the tenant's lease) would have
an expectation of at least thirty years' possession of the property.
So, if the tenant's immediate landlord only has a reversionary
interest of two years (that is, his lease expires two years after the
tenant's) the tenant must move up the chain to the next landlord
until he finds one who has a reversion of at least thirty years; or

(b) if nobody qualifies in paragraph (a) the reversioner is the owner
of the freehold interest.

However, the notice a sub-tenant has to give under the Act must be
served on his immediate landlord. The sub-tenant should also serve
the notice on any other superior landlord of whom he knows.

price
The existence of superior interests does not mean that a tenant
buying the freehold has to pay more for it. He simply buys out the
interests of each superior landlord separately. These interests are

valued on the basis of what they would fetch in a sale on the open market. Clearly the longer the reversion of a superior landlord, the more it is worth. But the sum total paid by the tenant should not normally exceed the amount he would have to pay if his landlord was the freeholder.

In one case the Act lays down a formula for calculating the price to be paid to a superior landlord; this is where the superior landlord's lease would expire within one month of the date of the occupying tenant's lease and the superior landlord's profit rent is not more than £5 per year. Profit rent is calculated by subtracting the rent paid to the superior landlord by his tenant from the rent paid by that superior landlord to his own landlord.

procedure

The Leasehold Reform Act lays down the procedure that must be followed by a landlord and tenant when a claim is made.

the tenant's notice

It is wise for the tenant to keep copies of any notices he sends, for future reference. A tenant must give the landlord notice of his intention to buy the freehold or claim an extended lease on form 1 *'Notice of leaseholder's claim'*. (If the notice is served by a sub-tenant, he should serve it on his own landlord and on anyone with a superior interest of whom he knows.) If the tenant is buying the freehold and knows that his landlord has a mortgage on the property, a copy of the notice should be served on the mortgagee.

Form 1 comprises 8 paragraphs, a schedule and 8 notes (referred to in the margin of the form).

In paragraph 1, the tenant must delete one of the two alternatives namely 'freehold' or 'extended lease'. A notice which does not state clearly which alternative the tenant is opting for will be invalid.

Paragraph 2 should be modified by the tenant by deleting one of the alternatives which appear in square brackets.

If a tenant knows that his landlord is the owner of the freehold, he may delete paragraphs 3 to 8 which apply only to claims by sub-tenants, and move on to complete the schedule.

The schedule to form 1 *Notice of leaseholder's claim* must contain information about the house sufficiently precise to identify all the property to which the claim extends; the rateable value of the house and premises on various dates; particulars of the tenancy; the date on which the tenant acquired the tenancy; the periods in the last 10 years during which the tenant has and has not occupied the house as his residence.

If a tenant cannot trace his landlord, he may apply to the High Court and they will advise him what to do. He will not lose his rights.

effect of tenant's notice
Unless the landlord successfully opposes the tenant's application, he is bound to convey the freehold to the tenant or grant him an extended lease. The notice, in effect, operates like a contract between the landlord and the tenant.

If a landlord has contracted to sell the freehold to a third party prior to his tenant claiming to buy the freehold, the tenant's rights are unaffected. The contract between the landlord and the third party disappears and the landlord must convey to the tenant.

withdrawing
Where the tenant is buying the freehold, once a price has been fixed, the tenant has a period of one month in which he may withdraw his notice. To withdraw, the must give notice in writing to his landlord (and all superior landlords if he is a sub-tenant). Such notice has the effect of cancelling the tenant's previous claim to buy the freehold. He must however pay any costs incurred by his landlord (or superior landlords).

the landlord's reply

Within 2 months of being served with a tenant's notice, a landlord (or, if the notice is served by a sub-tenant, the reversioner) must serve his notice in reply to the tenant. The form a landlord must use is form 2 (*Notice in reply to leaseholder's claim*). This form contains five paragraphs together with five explanatory notes (referred to in the margin of the form):

Paragraph 1: simply states that the landlord (or reversioner) has received a copy of the tenant's notice claiming to buy the freehold or extend his lease.

Paragraph 2: states whether the tenant's claim is admitted or not and if not, the grounds on which the landlord opposes the claim. A landlord who admits a tenant's claim cannot later dispute it unless he shows that the tenant has misled him in some way.

Paragraph 3: specifies whether any claim will be made to recover possession for the purposes of redevelopment or for the purpose of housing the landlord or an adult member of his family.

Paragraph 4: in certain circumstances a landlord can require the tenant to take additional premises or to exclude certain premises from his claim. A landlord here gives the tenant notice of this.

Paragraph 5: applies only to notices served by a reversioner where the tenant making the claim is a sub-tenant.

conveyancing procedure

The steps necessary to complete the conveyance or transfer of the freehold or the grant of an extended lease to a tenant are laid down in the Leasehold Reform (Enfranchisement and Extension) Regulations 1967. The procedure laid down by the Regulations may be varied by agreement.

Where a claim is made by a sub-tenant, the word landlord refers to the reversioner who conducts the sale or grant on behalf of superior landlords.

buying the freehold

(i) *Deposit:* At any time after receiving a tenant's notice a landlord may, in writing, ask the tenant to pay a deposit of either not more than £25 or three times the tenant's annual rent.

The tenant has 14 days in which to comply.

(ii) *Evidence of right to enfranchise:* The landlord may ask the tenant to prove his title to the tenancy and require the tenant to produce a statutory declaration giving details of his three years' occupation of the property. The tenant should ask a solicitor how to go about obtaining such a statutory declaration.

The tenant has 21 days to comply with the request.

(iii) *Proof of the landlord's title:* A tenant may, by notice in writing, require the landlord to deduce title to the freehold. This means that the landlord has to show who owns the freehold and whether or not it is subject to incumbrances. In the case of registered land, title is deduced by the landlord giving the tenant an authority to inspect the register, office copies of the entries on the register, and evidence of rights about which the register is not conclusive. (The procedure for buying and selling registered land is explained in the Consumer Publication *The legal side of buying a house*.) If title to the property is not registered, the landlord must provide the tenant with an abstract or epitome of his title. He should obtain the advice of a solicitor as to what the abstract or epitome should contain.

(iv) *Requisitions on title:* These are questions asked in writing by or on behalf of a buyer of property about the seller's ownership of it.

The tenant has to make his requisitions within 14 days of the date the landlord deduced title. The landlord must reply to the tenant's requisitions within 14 days of receiving them.

(v) *Contents and preparation of the transfer (registered land) or conveyance (unregistered land):* The Regulations specify time limits within which each party must let the other know of any provisions (such as to rights of way or restriction on the use of the property) to be included in the transfer or conveyance. The tenant may give the landlord notice asking him to specify any such provisions.

The landlord has 4 weeks in which to supply the relevant information. A landlord may similarly ask the tenant for details and the tenant has 4 weeks to reply.

The tenant has the task of preparing the transfer or conveyance. He must deliver a draft transfer or conveyance to the landlord (or his solicitor) at least 14 days before the date fixed for completion. The draft transfer or conveyance, when agreed, must be engrossed by the tenant and delivered to the landlord, a reasonable time before completion.

A tenant may be required to execute as many copies of the transfer or conveyance as the landlord reasonably requires.

(vi) *Completion:* After one month from the date on which the price the tenant has to pay has been determined, either the tenant or the landlord may give the other notice in writing requiring him to complete the transaction. The completion date is then set at the first working day after 4 weeks from the day of the notice have expired. Completion takes place at the office of the landlord's mortgagee's solicitor unless otherwise agreed.

If completion is delayed for any reason, the tenant must go on paying rent unless the landlord opts to take interest at 2% above the bank rate on the unpaid purchase money. Rent or interest remains payable until the day of actual completion.

Where completion is delayed solely because of the landlord's fault, the tenant may, instead:

○ at his own risk, deposit the price or the balance of the price, at any bank in England or Wales; and

○ give notice in writing of such deposit to the landlord or his solicitor.

The landlord has to accept such interest as is earned.

(vii) *Apportionment of rent and outgoings:* The tenant has to pay rent up to the date of actual completion and after that all outgoings, for instance rates. Any current rent and rates payable at the date of completion are to be apportioned on a daily basis.

(viii) *Time limits:* A reversioner may serve notice on the tenant specifying that the above time limits be doubled in so far as he is concerned: the time limits remain the same for the tenant.

(ix) *Failure to comply with obligations:* If either party fails to comply with his obligations, the other may serve a notice on the defaulting party giving him 2 months to make good his default.

If the tenant does not obey the notice, any deposit he has paid is forfeit, the landlord is released from his obligations and the tenant must pay the landlord's reasonable costs.

If the landlord is in default and does not comply with the notice, the tenant may recover his deposit and the landlord loses his right to recover his costs from the tenant. The tenant may then have to apply to the court if the landlord continues to be unhelpful.

claiming the grant of an extended lease

The procedure is much the same as for buying the freehold with obvious modifications to take account of the fact that only a 50-year lease is being granted.

There are, however, the following material differences:

(i) *Terms of the new tenancy:* Either party is required to state, by notice, what modifications (other than rent) are to be made to the terms of the existing tenancy. The landlord has the right to include restrictions on the use of the property in certain circumstances.

(ii) *Preparation of the lease:* Within 8 weeks of either party giving notice, the landlord must send a draft lease to the tenant who has 21 days to approve it with or without amendments. The landlord has to produce an engrossment of the lease and the required counterparts.

(iii) *Completion:*   When the time limit for the approval of the draft lease has elapsed, either party may serve notice in writing on the other, requiring completion of the lease. The completion date is then set as the first working day after the expiration of 4 weeks from the date notice is given.

costs

A tenant who exercises his rights under the Act has to meet the following items of expenditure:

○ The landlord's reasonable costs of investigating his right to the freehold or an extended lease.

○ The landlord's reasonable costs incurred in having a valuation of the house made; the cost of preparing the conveyance or transfer or lease.

○ The landlord's reasonable costs of deducing title to the freehold, where appropriate.

○ Stamp duty on the transfer or conveyance or lease, where appropriate (at present, where the purchase price is over £30,000).

○ Land Registry fees (for registered land only).

A landlord is entitled to refuse to execute a new, extended lease for a tenant unless:

(a) all rent due is paid; *and*

(b) all costs recoverable by the landlord are paid; *and*

(c) any other sums that are due to the landlord (for example service charges) are paid.

Where a sub-tenant exercises his rights under the Act, he is liable to pay the reasonable costs of all superior landlords, not just those of the reversioner.

Housing booklet No 9 *Leasehold Reform* published by the Department of the Environment and Welsh Office contains fifty questions and answers as a guide for leaseholders and landlords.

renting and letting in the public sector

Tenants in the public sector who are 'secure tenants' are given a number of rights by the Housing Act 1980 and the amending Housing and Building Control Act 1984. These include security of tenure, the right to buy their home, the right to be informed of their landlord's obligations under the tenancy, and other rights.

Basically, a secure tenant is someone (tenant or licensee) who rents from a designated landlord a dwelling-house which he uses as his only or main residence.

'designated' landlord
The landlord must be one of the following bodies:

○ a local housing authority, which includes district councils, London boroughs, the Greater London Council, metropolitan and city boroughs and the Council of the Isles of Scilly

○ the Commission for the New Towns

○ a development corporation (a statutory body set up to stimulate growth in new towns)

○ the Housing Corporation (Maple House, 149 Tottenham Court Road, London WIP 0BN, telephone 01-387 9466)

○ a county council

○ a housing trust which is a charity within the meaning of the Charities Act 1960 (The Charity Commissioners, telephone 01-214 6000, keep a register of all charities)

○ the Development Board for Rural Wales

○ a housing co-operative which is a company or body of trustees approved by the Secretary of State for the Environment as one which may exercise housing powers on behalf of a local authority

○ a housing association which satisfies one of the following conditions:

(a) it is registered with the Housing Corporation, or

(b) it applied for registration with the Housing Corporation before 1 April 1975, but has not yet been registered, or

(c) it has been the subject of an order made by the Secretary of State providing that regulations similar to those relating to local authorities shall apply, or

(d) the rules of the housing association state that its members must be tenants and its tenancies only available to members (so that a member tenant could not sell his tenancy to a non-member tenant). The housing association must also be registered under section 74 of the Industrial and Provident Societies Act 1965.

But where the housing association satisfies both condition (a) *and* condition (d), there cannot be a secure tenancy.

the dwelling-house
The tenancy (or licence) must be of accommodation let as a separate dwelling.

the tenant
The tenant (which includes a licensee) must be an individual or, where there is a joint tenancy, two or more individuals. A limited company cannot be a secure tenant.

The individual (or in a joint tenancy at least one of them) must occupy the dwelling-house as his only or principal home.

exceptions

The following tenancies or licences are not secure tenancies:

○ *long lease:* which is granted for 21 years or more even if it has a forfeiture clause which allows it to be ended earlier.

○ *service occupancy:* of an employee who is allowed to live in his employer's property by virtue of a lease or licence, so that he can better perform his work (even if the employer is one of the landlords listed above).

The Act mentions two types of employee in particular: a lease to a member of the police force, provided that it is free of rent and rates, does not create a secure tenancy. Similarly, a letting to an employee of a fire authority is not a secure tenancy, if the employee's contract stipulates that he must live near a particular fire station.

○ *students:* a letting by one of the designated landlords to a student who attends a full-time course at a university, polytechnic or other college is not normally a secure tenancy, but the landlord must give notice to the student explaining the exemption.

If a student's course finishes or he leaves it, the occupancy will become a secure tenancy after six months from the date the student's course finished or he left it. It is therefore important for the landlord to get possession as soon as he knows that either of these circumstances has arisen.

○ *business tenancies:* where a dwelling forms part of premises used mainly for business purposes; the tenancy (but not a licence) may, however, be protected by the Landlord and Tenant Act 1954.

○ *landlord with short-term interests:* any sub-tenancy created where the landlord is itself the tenant of a landlord or a body which is incapable of creating a secure tenancy and has a short-term interest only (but only if the head-landlord has the right to obtain vacant possession of the property at the end of the term or on giving notice).

○ *miscellaneous:* a licence granted by an almshouse charity whose constitution prevents the grant of leases; premises which have on-licences for the sale of drinks; lettings of agricultural holdings; a tenancy where a lease of a flat has been granted to a secure tenant who has exercised his right to extend a long lease by 50 years.

A secure tenant will cease to be secure if he gives up possession of the whole of his dwelling-house. This rule effectively prevents a secure tenant from sub-letting the whole of his home.

Where a tenant under a fixed term secure tenancy, granted before 5 November 1982, assigns his interest to his spouse or other person who is entitled to succeed to the tenancy on his death, the tenancy ceases to be secure (except where the assignment is made as a result of a property adjustment order on divorce).

temporary lettings
Local authorities have to give a homeless person temporary accommodation in certain circumstances, for example while it is decided whether that person should be the responsibility of another authority. Such a temporary letting is not initially a secure tenancy. But if the letting continues for more than 12 months after the local authority has finally decided, it will automatically become a secure tenancy.

A person who has moved into an area to find a job and permanent accommodation and is given temporary housing, will not usually be a secure tenant. If the letting continues for more than a year, however, it may become a secure tenancy. For this exemption to apply, the landlord must first give the jobseeker notice of the circumstances leading to the exemption.

Where a tenant, who was not a secure tenant, is let into temporary accommodation while work is carried out on his original dwelling-house, no secure tenancy is created.

Sometimes a public landlord will acquire property with a view to its re-development. If there is some delay before work on the property begins and the landlord lets it on a short-term basis in the interim period, no secure tenancy arises.

the rights of a secure tenant (including a licensee)

None of the tenant's rights can be excluded by the tenancy agreement.

the right to take in lodgers
A secure tenant may take in lodgers (unless by doing so the house becomes overcrowded), without obtaining the landlord's prior consent.

the right to sub-let
Every secure tenant has the right to sub-let part of his home. He must first obtain his landlord's consent, which cannot be unreasonably withheld. If the landlord refuses consent, the tenant can demand a written statement of the reasons for such refusal. If the landlord gives consent conditionally (for example, subject to the tenant doing certain repairs) the consent takes effect as though the condition did not exist. If the landlord neither gives nor refuses consent but merely remains silent, he will be deemed to have withheld consent unreasonably.

Where a secure tenant feels that his landlord has unreasonably refused consent or has remained silent, he should apply to the county court for a declaration of consent having been unreasonably withheld. He may then sub-let without risk of being in breach of the terms of his lease.

If a secure tenant sub-lets the whole of his home, he is no longer a secure tenant because he will not be in occupation of any part of the premises, and will lose the protection of the Housing Act.

the right to make improvements
This right is subject to first obtaining the landlord's written consent, which shall not be unreasonably withheld, but which may be given subject to reasonable conditions. Unless such conditions are complied with, the tenant will be treated as having broken a term of his lease.

A landlord is not allowed to increase the rent to take account of a tenant's improvements. Where the tenant pays rent inclusive of rates, however, he will have to bear the expense of any increase in rates resulting from the improvements. A secure tenant's successor is also protected from any increase in rent because of improvements made by his predecessor. Only when the successor's tenancy ends can the landlord increase the rent payable in respect of the improved property.

The 1980 Act gives public landlords a discretionary power to repay some or all of the cost of improvements to a secure tenant. The power exists only where the improvement was made after 3 October 1980, the landlord gave written consent and the improvement materially added to the price which the property would be expected to fetch if sold or rented in the open market. The landlord is under no duty to make such payments.

the right to carry out the landlord's repairing obligations and recover the cost
The landlord's obligations to repair may be contained in the lease. Whatever the tenancy agreement says, the landlord must honour its obligations under the Housing Act 1961. Certain repairs are almost always the council's responsibility. They include:

○ repairs to the structure of the building such as roof, walls, floors and windows;

○ upkeep of the outside of the building such as gutters, pipes and drains;

○ plumbing and sanitary conveniences such as baths, w.c., sinks and basins;

○ electrical wiring, gas piping, fixed heaters and water heaters.

The SHAC guide for council tenants *Your rights to repair* deals with getting the council to do repairs and the tenant getting the work done himself.

The Housing and Building Control Act 1984 inserted a new provision into the 1980 Housing Act to give secure tenants the right to carry out repairs which should have been done by their landlord, and to recover from the landlord the cost of the repairs. Alternatively, he may ask the landlord to pay the cost directly. The draft *Right to repair* regulations under the Act, give council tenants the right to have repairs costing between £20 and £200 carried out by themselves, or by a builder at their local council's expense – provided the council agreed first. The exact details of the provision have yet to be decided by the Secretary of State, and it is not yet known how it will work out in practice.

The 1984 Act does not affect a tenant's common law right to sue a landlord for damages for breach of repairing obligation.

the right to exchange
All secure tenants may exchange their homes with other secure tenants. There is no need for the two secure tenants to have the same landlord. Obtaining the landlord's consent is a pre-condition to exchange; where the secure tenants have different landlords, the consent of both landlords is required.

The landlord may refuse consent only on one of the grounds listed below, and must give his tenant notice of such refusal within 42 days of the tenant applying for consent.

Consent to exchange can be refused if:

o a possession order has been made, or possession proceedings have been started, against the landlord's existing tenant or the person with whom he wants to exchange ('the tenant by way of exchange') on one of the grounds relating to a tenant's default under his lease (failure to pay rent, damage to furniture and so on)

o the tenant by way of exchange would have substantially more accommodation than he reasonably requires or the accommodation is too small for his and his family's needs

o the dwelling-house is let by a charity and occupation by the proposed tenant by way of exchange would result in a breach of the charity's objects

o the landlord is a housing association or housing trust which lets the property only to people whose circumstances (other than financial circumstances) make them difficult to house and the exchange would mean that such a person would no longer live in the property

○ the property is specially adapted for a physically disabled person and the result of the exchange would be that such a person would no longer occupy the property

○ the property is one of a group set up for people with special needs near to specially provided facilities or social services and the exchange would mean the property would no longer be occupied by a person with such special needs

○ the property is within the curtilage of a building held by a landlord for non-residential purposes and is let to an employee of either the landlord or a local authority, new town or urban development corporation, Commission for the New Towns, county council, governors of an aided school or the Development Board for Rural Wales, and the employee holds his secure tenancy in consequence of his employment (if the employee occupies the property for the better fulfilment of his job, he does not have a secure tenancy, only a service occupancy).

A secure tenant should not take any lump sum payment on exchange. If he does, the landlord may be able to recover possession and would not have to provide alternative accommodation.

the right to information
A secure tenant can require his landlord to furnish him with a full and simple explanation of the terms of his tenancy and his rights under the 1980 Act. The landlord must include details of its repairing obligations under the lease and under the Housing Act 1961. Furthermore, the landlord must publish its procedure for allocating accommodation and allowing transfers. The rules for allocating houses and transfers/exchanges must be available for tenants to read (free of charge). Summaries of the schemes should be available free of charge and, for a small fee, copies of the full set of rules.

There is the new right of allowing tenants (or 'any person who has applied for housing accommodation') to see, without charge, details of the particulars which he has given to the authority and which the authority has recorded as being relevant to his application.

The Housing and Building Control Act 1984 also gives a secure tenant the right to ask for information regarding charges made in respect of heating and the supply of hot water, where this is made in accordance with a local scheme. The exact scope of the right has yet to be determined by the Secretary of State.

the right to be consulted
The secure tenant has the right to be consulted by his landlord on most aspects of housing management. If a landlord proposes to make substantial alterations to the layout of an estate, for instance, the tenants must be consulted, and their views considered before a decision is taken. Landlords must, on request, provide their secure tenants with details of their consultation procedure.

Similarly, a landlord may not vary the terms of a secure tenancy, except

o by agreement with the tenant;

o in accordance with the terms of the tenancy in relation to payments for rent, rates and services; or

o by notice of variation in the case of a periodic secure tenancy. The landlord serves notice of the variation on the tenant, explaining the substance of the variation and asking the tenant for his comments. After considering the tenant's comments, the landlord serves a further notice of variation which states the date on which the variation is to take effect: this must be either when a rental period expires or after four weeks, whichever is longer. The tenant's sole remedy, if he objects to the variation, is to give notice to quit. The landlord does not need to observe the procedure of a preliminary notice when issuing a variation notice regarding payments in respect of rent, rates or services.

security of tenure

Secure tenants enjoy security of tenure analogous to that of private sector regulated tenants under the Rent Act 1977. The tenant may go on living in his home after his contractual right to be there has ended and the landlord needs a court order to regain possession which will be granted only in certain prescribed circumstances.

the right to remain in possession
When a secure tenant's original periodic tenancy or fixed-term tenancy or licence agreement comes to an end, he becomes entitled to a statutory periodic tenancy: he continues on the same terms as the original secure tenancy in so far as these terms are compatible with a periodic tenancy. The notional length of the periodic tenancy will depend on how the tenant has been paying rent: if monthly, the periodic tenancy will be a monthly one; if weekly there will be a weekly periodic tenancy and so on.

If the secure tenant was originally a periodic tenant there will be little change in his position, except that the landlord's right to end the new statutory periodic tenancy by notice to quit is restricted.

successors
If a secure tenant dies (before or after the end of the original occupation agreement), generally the tenancy is automatically transferred to the person entitled to succeed to the secure tenancy under the 1980 Act. But unlike statutory tenancies under the Rent Act, there is only one automatic successor; nothing in the Act, however, prevents a landlord from agreeing to a second succession.

A person may succeed a secure tenant if at the time of the secure tenant's death he/she occupied the dwelling-house as his or her only or principal home and is either

○ the secure tenant's husband or wife; or

○ another member of the secure tenant's family and has lived with the secure tenant throughout the 12 months up to the secure tenant's death.

The other members of the secure tenant's family are: the so-called 'common-law' husband or wife, parents, grandparents, grandchildren, children, brothers and sisters, uncles and aunts, nephews and nieces; relations by marriage, illegitimate children and adopted children are also included.

A secure tenant's spouse takes precedence over other members of the family. If two or more members of the family are entitled to succeed to the secure tenancy and cannot agree between themselves who is to take it, the landlord can decide who is to be the successor.

no successors

In the following circumstances there will be no automatic transfer on the death of the secure tenant:

○ where there has already been an automatic transfer to a secure tenant's spouse or a member of his family; or

○ where the deceased secure tenant acquired the tenancy under the will or on the intestacy of the previous tenant; or

○ on the death of a surviving joint tenant (where there is a joint tenancy and one tenant dies, the tenancy automatically passes to the survivor under the general law); or

○ where there was originally a fixed term or periodic tenancy which has been assigned (sold or exchanged). Although the assignee will be statutorily entitled to a periodic tenancy when the original term ends, there is no automatic transfer on his death.

Assignees who take over the secure tenancy under a property transfer order on or after divorce, nullity or judicial separation, do not count as assignees for this purpose. However, if the other party to the marriage had acquired the tenancy by assignment there will be no rights of succession.

how to end a secure tenancy

Basically, there are four ways in which a secure tenancy can be ended:

1   agreement between the landlord and tenant;

2   the secure tenant exercising his 'right to buy';

3   the landlord obtaining a court order enforcing a right to forfeit his tenant's lease and re-enter the property. (However, a periodic tenancy would automatically arise and the tenant would not have to move out unless the landlord obtains a court order for possession);

4   a landlord obtaining an order for possession from the court. Before the court will grant such an order, a landlord must establish one of the grounds for possession listed in the Housing Act (as amended).

A landlord who wishes to obtain a court order for possession must first serve on the tenant notice in the prescribed form. There are two forms: one for use where the secure tenant has a periodic tenancy, the other for use where the landlord wants to end a fixed term tenancy under a proviso for re-entry and forfeiture and regain possession.

Both state the name(s) of the secure tenant(s), the name of the landlord and address of the property, the ground on which possession is sought and the landlord's reasons for taking action to recover possession. There are extensive notes to explain the importance of the notice to the recipient. A notice in respect of a periodic tenancy also gives a date before which court proceedings cannot be brought.

the statutory grounds for obtaining possession

The Housing Act 1980 (as amended) lays down the grounds on which a landlord may recover possession.

reasonableness
The court will grant an order for possession on any one of the following grounds if it is reasonable to do so. (The court must consider reasonableness separately from the grounds.)

GROUND I: Any rent lawfully due from a tenant has not been paid, or any obligation (such as to repair) has been broken or not performed. A tenant may avoid a possession order if he makes good his breach of covenant or pays off all arrears of rent before court proceedings start. Mostly councils do not want to obtain possession but to get the arrears back. So, orders are often suspended, pending the payment of the arrears at so-much per week in addition to current rent. (But even if the full amount of the arrears is paid off, the tenant may still be liable for the costs of the local authority in bringing the action unless they agree not to proceed with it.)

GROUND II: The tenant or any person living with him has been guilty of conduct which constitutes a nuisance or annoyance to neighbours or has been convicted of using the dwelling-house (or allowing it to be used) for immoral or illegal purposes.

GROUND III: The condition of the dwelling-house or any of the common parts has deteriorated due to the act or default (for example, not carrying out repairs) of the tenant or any person living with him. If the tenant has a lodger or sub-tenant who has caused the deterioration, the landlord has to show that the tenant has not taken reasonable steps to remove the lodger or sub-tenant.

GROUND IV: The tenant or someone living with him has damaged furniture provided by the landlord. Again, if the furniture has been damaged by a lodger or sub-tenant, the landlord has to show that the tenant has not taken reasonable steps to remove him.

GROUND V: The tenant induced the landlord to grant him the tenancy by making false statements.

GROUND Va: The tenant has exchanged and a premium was paid either to or by him, by or to the other party.

GROUND Vb: The landlord is one of the following bodies

- a local authority
- a new town or urban development corporation
- the Commission for the New Towns
- a county council
- the governors of an aided school
- the Development Board for Rural Wales

and the tenant's dwelling-house is part of property used mainly for non-residential purposes and the tenant's conduct or that of a person living with him makes it wrong for him to continue to occupy. In this case, the tenancy must have been originally granted as a result of his employment with the landlord.

GROUND VI: The tenant occupies (or the previous tenant occupied) the dwelling-house while works are (or were) executed on his previous home and

o he (or the previous tenant) was a secure tenant of the previous home; and

○ he (or the previous tenant) promised to leave the present premises when the works on his previous home were finished; and

○ the works are now finished.

alternative accommodation

A landlord may obtain a court order for possession on one of the following grounds, if suitable alternative accommodation will be available to the tenant when the order is to take effect.

Alternative accommodation is suitable if it is let on a secure or protected tenancy and, in the opinion of the court, reasonably suitable to the needs of the tenant and his family. In determining this the court must have regard to

○ the nature of the accommodation which the landlord in practice allocates to someone with similar needs;

○ the distance of the accommodation from the workplace or school/college, and so on, of the tenant and any members of his family;

○ the distance of the accommodation from the home of any member of the tenant's family where being near is essential to the well-being of either the tenant or the member of his family;

○ the extent of the accommodation and the means of the tenant and his family;

○ the terms on which the accommodation is available and the terms of the secure tenancy;

○ where furniture is provided under the secure tenancy, whether it is to be provided for the tenant in the alternative accommodation and, if so, the nature of that furniture.

Where the landlord is not a local authority and produces a certificate from the local authority saying that they will provide suitable accommodation, this is conclusive that such accommodation will be available. Local authorities are normally reluctant to give such certificates.

The grounds for possession are:

GROUND VII: The dwelling-house is overcrowded within the meaning of the Housing Act 1957.

GROUND VIII: The landlord intends, within a reasonable time of obtaining possession, to demolish or reconstruct the building or carry out work on the building (or on land let with it) and cannot reasonably do so without obtaining possession of the secure tenant's home. There must be a firm intention to redevelop on the part of the landlord, not merely some vague plan for the future. The court might, for example, ask the landlord to produce builders' estimates.

GROUND IX: The landlord is a charity and the tenant's continued occupation of the property conflicts with the objects of the charity.

reasonableness and alternative accommodation
To obtain possession on one of the following grounds, the landlord must satisfy the court not only that it is reasonable to make an order for possession but also that suitable alternative accommodation will be available to the tenant when the order becomes effective.

GROUND IXa: The tenant was formerly an employee of the landlord (or one of the bodies specified in GROUND vb) and the dwelling-house is within the curtilage of a building consisting mainly of accommodation held by the landlord for non-housing purposes and is reasonably needed for one of its employees (or an employee of one of the specified bodies) in the future.

GROUND X: The tenant occupies property specifically adapted for use by a physically disabled person, there is no longer a disabled person living there, and the landlord wants possession for occupation by such a person.

GROUND XI: The landlord is a housing association which lets only to people whose circumstances (other than financial) make it especially difficult for them to satisfy their need for housing, there is now no longer anyone with special circumstances living in the property or the present tenant has received a firm offer of suitable alternative accommodation from a local authority, and the premises are required to house someone with special circumstances.

GROUND XII: The dwelling-house is one of a group which the landlord lets to people with special needs, *and*

a social service or special facility is provided in close proximity to assist the tenants, *and* the dwelling-house is not occupied by a person with special needs, *and*

the landlord requires the property for a person with special needs to live in.

So, a landlord who lets houses in a complex specially designed for the elderly may regain possession on this ground.

GROUND XIII: The tenant has succeeded to the secure tenancy and the property is more extensive than is reasonably required by him. The court must take account of the tenant's age, the length of occupation of the dwelling, and any financial or other support given by the tenant to the previous tenant. To recover possession on this ground, the landlord must bring proceedings between six and twelve months from the death of the previous tenant. A spouse of the deceased tenant cannot be dispossessed on this ground.

the right to buy

A secure tenant who can satisfy three conditions – the landlord condition, the tenant condition and the time condition – has the right to buy his home.

the landlord condition
The landlord must be one of the following bodies:

○ a local authority or county council

○ the Commission for the New Towns

○ the Development Board for Rural Wales

○ a development corporation

○ the Housing Corporation

○ a housing co-operative approved as such by the Secretary of State

○ a housing association which is registered with the Housing Corporation (or which applied to be registered before 1 April 1975 and its application is pending), or one which has been the subject of an order made by the Secretary of State stating that provisions similar to those applicable to local authorities shall apply. Housing associations which are also charities registered under the Industrial and Provident Societies Act 1965, or which have never received public funds to subsidise their activities, are expressly excluded.

The landlord must also own the freehold, or be in a position to grant a lease for over 21 years in the case of a house, or fifty years in the case of a flat.

the tenant condition ('tenant' includes licensee)
The tenant's immediate landlord must be one of those listed above; sub-tenants at present do not fall within the right to buy provisions. However, the Secretary of State may extend the scheme to cover certain secure sub-tenants, namely those whose own landlords are themselves tenants of right-to-buy landlords.

If the tenant is an undischarged bankrupt or has had a possession order made against him, he will not be able to exercise the right to buy his home. Tenants who are in arrears with their rent must bring the payment up to date before they can exercise their right to buy.

the time condition
The tenant must have been a tenant of a public sector landlord for at least 2 years. The two-year period does not need to be spent in the same dwelling or as a tenant of the same landlord.

Time spent by the tenant's spouse (or ex-spouse or deceased spouse) as a public sector tenant or armed forces occupier usually counts towards the two years.

joint tenants and members of the family
When two or more secure joint tenants are entitled to buy their home, the right belongs to them all jointly. At least one of these joint tenants must occupy the dwelling as his only or principal home.

A secure tenant may, when he gives notice of his intention to buy, require that up to 3 members of his family (who need not be joint tenants) be allowed to buy with him. The secure tenant can join his spouse or any member of the family who lives and has for the past 12 months lived with him, or – if the family member has not lived with the tenant – if the landlord gives his consent to the family member joining in the purchase.

what a secure tenant can buy

A secure tenant of a house can buy the freehold interest, provided that the landlord owns the freehold. In other cases, the tenant will be granted a long lease (over twenty-one years) of the house. This normally means that he may buy the freehold under the Leasehold Reform Act 1967.

buying a long lease
The secure tenant of a flat is entitled to buy a long lease of the flat. The minimum term of the lease will be fifty years, usually it is for much longer; where the landlord is a freeholder, the normal minimum is 125 years. Where the landlord does not own the freehold, its interest must be sufficient to support these sub-leases – in fact, the lease bought should be landlord's interest minus 5 days.

The following provisions will be contained (or implied) in the lease:

o rights to the enjoyment of common parts previously enjoyed by the secure tenant

o that the landlord will keep the structure and exterior of the dwelling-house in repair and make good any defect affecting that structure, unless details of such defects have been given to the tenant

o indemnity by the tenant in respect of breach of restrictive covenants affecting the landlord

o covenant by the tenant to keep the interior in good repair

o rights of support, passage of water, gas, electricity, etc

o necessary rights of way

o other rights enjoyed by the tenant when he gave notice of intent to buy, insofar as the landlord can grant them.

Some of these rights (such as the last three) will also be included in a conveyance of the freehold to a secure tenant who is exercising his right to buy, where appropriate.

'shared ownership'

The Housing and Building Control Act 1984 introduces an alternative for secure tenants who have established, but cannot afford to exercise, their right to buy – for instance, whose mortgage entitlement, under the right to buy, is insufficient to enable them to buy outright. They can require the landlord to grant a shared-ownership lease of the dwelling-house.

Broadly speaking, the tenant initially buys a 50% (or $62\frac{1}{2}$% or 75% or $89\frac{1}{2}$%) interest in the property. He then increases his stake by buying a further $12\frac{1}{2}$% (or multiples of $12\frac{1}{2}$%) stakes in the property, until he owns the whole interest. Throughout the period during which he owns only part of the interest of the house or flat, he continues to pay the landlord rent (calculated according to a statutory formula, based on the proportion owned by the tenant, so that usually the rent is substantially less than the rent he was paying before he bought an interest in the property).

Before a secure tenant can claim a shared-ownership lease, he must have applied for a right-to-buy mortgage and been told that he is entitled to less than a 100% mortgage. He must also have served a notice on the landlord deferring completion of the purchase, and put down a minimum deposit of £100.

no right to buy
Certain types of dwelling-house are not within the right to buy provision:

○ accommodation classed as 'sheltered', which is used to provide homes for elderly people

○ accommodation specially designed or adapted for disabled people

○ accommodation similar in character to that in 'GROUND vb'

○ local authority properties held under non-housing powers and let to their employees for the better performance of their duties (this must be stated in their contracts of employment).

A detailed booklet issued by the Department of the Environment and the Welsh Office *Your right to buy your home* includes notes on shared ownership, as does the Department of the Environment housing booklet No 15 *Shared Ownership* which includes a step by step guide.

calculating the price
The Housing Act 1980 lays down the method for calculating the price a secure tenant must pay when buying his home. The formula is:

**value of dwelling-house at relevant time
minus discount entitlement**

the value of the dwelling-house
This is the price which it would realise if sold on the open market by a willing seller, at the relevant time. In the case of a sale of the freehold interest, the following assumptions are made:

○ the vendor is selling the freehold with vacant possession;

○ neither the tenant nor a member of his family living there with him wants to buy;

○ the property is to be conveyed subject only to rights and burdens which may be imposed under the Housing Act 1980. These include necessary rights of way, rights of support and light and passage of water, gas and electricity, sewage and so on.

On the grant of a long lease (flat, or a house where the landlord is himself a leaseholder) the assumptions are that:

○ the ground rent will not exceed £10 per annum;

○ where the landlord has an interest of more than 125 years plus 5 days, he is granting a lease of 125 years with vacant possession;

○ where the landlord has an interest of less than 125 years and 5 days, he is granting a lease equal to the remainder of his own term less 5 days, with vacant possession;

○ neither the tenant nor a member of his family living there with him wants to take the lease;

○ the grant is on the terms specified in the Housing Act 1980.

The effect of these assumptions is to lower the price which the property would otherwise realise if sold to the secure tenant.

In making the valuation, any improvements made by the secure tenant or a member of his family or predecessors (if they would have been secure tenants) are ignored.

In the first instance, it is the responsibility of the landlord to determine the value of the dwelling-house at the relevant time. A landlord may ask the district valuer to help him in this respect. If the district valuer is not initially consulted, or the tenant disagrees with the value attributed to the dwelling by the landlord or the district valuer, the tenant has the right to require a revaluation to be carried out by another officer from the district valuer's office. A tenant must serve written notice on his landlord within 3 months of receiving his landlord's valuation, requiring the district valuer's involvement. (Standard forms for this are available from law stationers.)

the relevant time
This is the date on which the secure tenant serves notice of his intention to buy.

discount entitlement

This is based on the length of time the secure tenant has been a secure tenant.

period to be taken into account	discount (% of value at relevant time)
Two years or more	32% plus 1% for each complete year in excess of 2 years

Let us assume that Mr Samuel Taylor has lived in his council house for 10 years and at the date he makes his application it is valued at £20,000. He will pay £20,000 less £8,000 (discount of 40%) amounting to £12,000.

The periods to be taken into account in calculating the discount entitlement are the same as those which count towards the two-year residence requirement.

The maximum amount of discount which may be claimed is whichever of the following is the least:

(i) £25,000 (this figure may be changed in the future by the Secretary of State); or

(ii) 60% of the value of the dwelling-house; or

(iii) a figure which would not result in the tenant paying less for his home than it cost the landlord to build, buy or improve, where these costs were incurred after 1 April 1974.

losing the discount

A secure tenant's discount will be reduced if he has bought previously and received a discount on that occasion. Similarly, the discount will be reduced where the tenant's spouse or other joint purchaser has received discount on a prior occasion.

A secure tenant who buys his home at discount and then sells it to a third party within the next five years is liable to repay some or all of the discount he received. This applies to most sales, assignments and sub-lettings for a period of more than twenty-one years. But a

disposal to a spouse or resident members of the family who have
lived with the tenant for a year or more is exempt from these
provisions, and so are disposals by will, or on a divorce following a
court order, or disposals to someone who could have bought (or does
buy) compulsorily, or disposals of part of the property not including
the residential part.

The amount to be repaid depends on when the sale, assignment or
sub-letting takes place:

sale made	discount repayable
in the first year	100%
in the second year	80%
in the third year	60%
in the fourth year	40%
in the fifth year	20%

So, if Mr Samuel Taylor tries to make a quick profit by selling his
house in the second year after he bought it, he will be liable to repay
£6,400. The obligation to repay takes effect as if the landlord had a
legal mortgage over the property for the amount of the discount.
This 'mortgage' ranks in priority after the council mortgage or any
charge securing money borrowed by the tenant from the Housing
Corporation, any building society, bank or insurance company to
finance the right to buy. A landlord should immediately protect his
charge (against a sale by the tenant within the five year period) by
registering a caution or notice at the Land Registry.

In some cases, a secure tenant does not have an unrestricted right to
sell after 5 years. In certain rural areas, in particular areas of
outstanding natural beauty and National Parks, there are restrictions
on the persons to whom a secure tenant who has bought his home
may sell it – for example, only to someone who lives or works in the
area. In these areas, the possibility of such a restriction is taken into
account in valuing the house or flat at the relevant time.

choosing the time for buying and selling

It is not necessarily in the best interests of the tenant to serve a notice of intention to exercise his rights to buy at the earliest opportunity, because for every extra year he waits he will get an extra 1% discount. For example, on a property valued at £50,000 this means an extra £500 discount every year.

A tenant should therefore be aware of the precise date on which his qualifying occupation began, because it could be a matter of only days, whether or not he gets an extra 1% discount.

Against this have to be weighed two factors: first, the valuation is on the date the tenant serves his notice of intention to buy, and property prices usually rise by more than 1% a year. So, while it may be worth an intending tenant waiting just a few days, it may not be worthwhile for say, something approaching a year. Second, the longer a tenant waits to exercise his right, the later will be the date when the discount he has to repay to the landlord on any future sale is reduced.

As for selling, the tenant should, within the first five years, consider carefully whether he should wait until the expiration of a further year before selling. Every time a year expires since the date the purchase was completed, Mr Samuel Taylor would have to repay £1,600 less to the landlord on any sale.

the procedure

STEP I
The tenant serves *Notice Claiming the Right to Buy* on his landlord (form RTB1). The landlord has to supply form RTB1 within 7 days of receiving a request for it.

Form RTB1 comprises seven sections asking for details of the property, the landlord, the tenant and members of the tenant's family who wish to share the right to buy; the periods of occupation which will count towards calculating the discount; any previous purchase at a discount from one of the public sector landlords; particulars of any improvements made to the property.

STEP II

Within 4 weeks of receiving form RTB1, the landlord must serve *Notice in Reply to Tenant's Right to Buy Claim* (form RTB2). The period is 8 weeks if the two-year qualifying period includes a period as the tenant of a different landlord.

On form RTB2, the landlord inserts the names of those secure tenants whose claim to buy he admits, and of those whose claim he denies, with the reasons for denying the claim.

If a landlord denies the tenant's claim, the tenant should go to a citizens' advice bureau or legal aid centre and seek legal advice. If his efforts are unsuccessful, he can still go to the county court to try and establish his rights.

STEP III

If the landlord admits the tenant's claim or the tenant successfully establishes his right, the landlord must send the tenant a notice stating the proposed terms of sale. The notice must be served by the landlord within 8 weeks of the service of form RTB2 (in the case of a freehold purchase) or 12 weeks (in cases where a lease is being granted). The notice must state:

o the price, and how it was calculated

o the discount entitlement, and how this was calculated

o tenant's improvements which have been disregarded

o provisions to be included in the conveyance or lease; if the landlord is to grant a lease and there will be a service charge, an estimate of that charge

o in the case of flats only, details of any structural defect which the tenant will be responsible for repairing when he exercises the right to buy, and what will be the tenant's share of the cost of putting right the defect; this will have been taken into account in the valuation

o details of the tenant's right to mortgage (an application form must be included)

○ details of the shared ownership lease scheme

○ details of the notice to complete procedure.

no delays

The landlord has to deal with the completion of the conveyance or grant of the lease as quickly as circumstances allow. Naturally, the tenant's mortgage arrangements must be finalised and the terms of the lease agreed but, after that, if the landlord unreasonably delays, the tenant can ask the Secretary of State to exercise his default powers to push through the conveyance or grant of a lease.

Where a secure tenant claims a mortgage and this is not enough to meet all the costs of his purchase, he may be able to defer completion of the sale. The tenant must serve on the landlord notice of his wish to defer completion until he can find the extra money to meet all his costs, within 3 months of receiving his mortgage offer. He must also pay a deposit of £100. The deposit is returnable if the sale does not go ahead. The maximum time for which completion may be postponed is 2 years from the date of service of form RTB1. By doing so, he may then also qualify for the right to buy on shared-ownership terms instead.

If the tenant delays completing after certain time limits have elapsed, the landlord can serve the tenant with a notice requiring him to state whether the delay is due to outstanding matters in respect of a mortgage or grant of a lease. The tenant is given a reasonable time (at least 56 days) in which to reply. The landlord's notice also states what will happen to the tenant's claim if he fails to comply with a notice to complete, should the landlord subsequently serve one.

No notice requiring an explanation for delay can be served:

○ where the value of the dwelling remains to be finally determined (an example would be where the tenant has asked for a determination by the district valuer)

○ if the tenant has not claimed a mortgage, unless nine months have passed since he first could have claimed the mortgage

○ during any period in which the tenant has exercised his right to defer completion

○ while the tenant is claiming a shared-ownership lease.

If the landlord gets no reasonable explanation for the delay, he may serve a notice on the tenant to complete within the period stated in the notice. This must be a reasonable period, with a minimum of 56 days, and the period can be extended by the landlord. If the tenant does not complete within the stated time, he is treated as having withdrawn his claim to buy his home.

A notice to complete cannot be served on a tenant who claims a shared-ownership lease.

withdrawing a claim
A secure tenant may withdraw his claim at any time by giving written notice (forms are available from law stationers) to his landlord. Theoretically, he may withdraw his claim one day and put in a new claim the next.

cost to the tenant

The tenant usually has to meet the following expenses in addition to the purchase price:

○ His own costs of employing a surveyor and/or solicitor. A tenant is not liable for any legal or other professional fees incurred by the landlord, other than a maximum of £50 in connection with a mortgage provided by the landlord. If his mortgage is from some independent source, he will have to pay the legal costs in connection with it.

○ Stamp duty at the rate of 1% of the price paid where the purchase price is more than £30,000.

○ Land Registry fees, because a tenant who buys his home under the Housing Act has to register his title with the appropriate District

Land Registry. The fee depends on the value of the property. The Land Registry procedure (described fully in the Consumer Publication *The legal side of buying a house*) is simplified for right to buy sales.

the right to a mortgage

A secure tenant who has the right to buy, has the right to obtain a mortgage to finance the purchase, usually from his landlord. However, where the tenant's landlord is a housing association, the mortgage is provided by the Housing Corporation.

Where two or more tenants have the right to buy, a mortgage can be obtained jointly by all of them. By pooling their income they may be able to get a larger mortgage than a sole secure tenant.

The tenant and landlord may agree on the terms of a mortgage (although there is a limit on the amount that can be borrowed). Where there is no such agreement, the following terms will apply.

how much can be borrowed
The final amount advanced will depend on income (in the case of joint application, aggregate incomes).

The applicant's annual income must first be calculated from all sources, minus, where applicable, an amount equal to any payments made under a maintenance agreement, court order or credit agreement, provided these payments are likely to continue for the next 18 months or more. Deducting these sums from annual income gives the tenant's 'available annual income'. This is then multiplied by a number which depends on his age at the time he gives notice of wanting to exercise the right to buy. The appropriate multiplier is

age on giving notice	multiplier
under 60	2.5
60–64	2.0
65 and over	1.0

So – if Mr Marks (who is under 60) has an annual income of £11,200 and pays £100 per month HP for a car, his mortgage entitlement would be:

	£
annual income	11,200
less annual credit payments	1,200
available annual income	10,000

mortgage advance = £10,000 × 2.5 = £25,000

Where two or more joint tenants have the right to buy, they must first decide whose annual income is to be treated as the principal income. The calculation for that tenant is as described above, then a figure for the other's available annual income is calculated and this amount added to the principal income earner. So if Mr Marks' wife had an available annual income of £2,500, their joint mortgage entitlement would be £27,500.

the term
The term of the mortgage over which the secure tenant should repay is 25 years, but he may opt for a shorter term or the landlord may extend his term. If the tenant buys a leasehold interest of less than 25 years, the mortgage term will be shorter, of course.

interest rate
The Housing Act specifies the rate of interest chargeable where a secure tenant buys from a county council, district council or London borough, the Greater London Council, the Common Council of the City of London or the Council of the Isles of Scilly. The rate is the higher of the standard rate as declared by the Secretary of State, or the applicable local average rate (broadly speaking $\frac{1}{4}$% above the rate paid by the local authority to borrow the money to provide to a secure tenant). However, the Secretary of State may give a local authority written notice containing a rate at which interest must be charged on such mortgages.

A secure tenant who buys from a landlord other than one of those detailed above should write to the landlord for an estimate of the initial interest rate.

The interest rate may vary during the mortgage term regardless of who the landlord is.

how to apply for a mortgage under the Act
A secure tenant buying from a housing association claims a mortgage by serving notice in the prescribed form on the Housing Corporation (149 Tottenham Court Road, London W1P 0BN). All other secure tenants serve notice claiming a mortgage on their landlords.

The prescribed form is *Notice Claiming The Right to a Mortgage* (form No 4). It must be sent to a tenant by his landlord along with the notice of terms of sale.

Form 4 asks for details of a secure tenant's income, commitments to be deducted in calculating available annual income and, in the case of joint tenants, it asks whose income is to be treated as the principal income.

The form must be served on the landlord (or Housing Corporation if appropriate) within 3 months of receiving the landlord's notice of terms of sale or the determination of the value of the house by the district valuer where the value is disputed. The period may be extended if there are reasonable grounds for so doing.

A landlord or the Housing Corporation must reply to a tenant's claim on form 4 'as soon as practicable'. The reply must state:

○ the amount which in the opinion of the landlord or the Housing Corporation the tenant is entitled to have advanced;

○ the method used to calculate the amount;

○ the provisions which the landlord or the Housing Corporation feels should be included in the mortgage deed.

A statement must accompany the landlord's (or Housing Corporation's) reply, informing the tenant of his rights to defer completion or take a shared ownership lease if the tenant's income does not qualify him for a full 100% mortgage.

other sources of finance
Nothing precludes a secure tenant from seeking a mortgage from sources other than his landlord (or the Housing Corporation) to finance his right to buy, but the tenant has no right to a mortgage from building societies, banks, insurance companies and so on. The availability of a mortgage from the landlord may be important to an older tenant, say above 50 years, because many other lenders may not be prepared to lend to a person of that age.

glossary

abstract
a summary of the proof of a person's ownership of land prepared from the title deeds and other documents

act of parliament
a law made by parliament; a statute

action
process by which one person seeks the help of the civil court to enforce a right against another

agent
person who has authority to act on behalf of another

assignment
sale or transfer of the whole of a tenant's interest in a lease to another person

common law
the traditional law of England and Wales, derived from custom and judges' interpretation (as against statute law)

completion
the final stage of the legal transaction when buying or selling a freehold or leasehold

contract
a legally binding agreement; can be oral, but where it concerns land it should be evidenced in writing

controlled rent
rent in which the maximum level is limited by law

covenant
a promise between landlord and tenant whereby they are bound to
do certain things, such as to pay the rent or to repair; may be express
or implied

county court
court which deals with small civil cases, including landlord's and
tenant's (generally, the amount at stake must not be more than
£5,000)

criminal law
the part of the law which punishes behaviour harmful to the
community as a whole, as against the civil law which confers rights
and duties on individual people

curtilage
piece of ground (such as a courtyard) or part of a building near to
and belonging to a house

deed
a document which is 'signed, sealed and delivered'; the seal need not
be wax but can be a small round paper disc; delivery is physically
handing over with the intention of making it operative (the transfer
of the legal title to leasehold property has to be by deed)

demised premises
property which is the subject matter of a lease with certain implied
covenants, such as promising that the tenant shall have quiet
enjoyment of the premises

determination
when an interest in land comes to an end or ceases

disposition
any transferring of an interest in land, for example a sale, a gift, a
lease, or by will

enfranchisement
tenant with long lease buying the freehold of the property under the
Leasehold Reform Act 1967

engross
formally to prepare an agreed draft document for execution

equitable interest
rights in a property which fall short of legal title, for example where a lease is not properly created it may be an equitable lease

estate
person's interest in land (may be freehold or leasehold)

execute
to sign, seal and deliver a document

exclusive possession
the right to keep all others out of premises, including the landlord

forfeiture
the means by which a landlord can bring a lease to an early end following a breach of covenant by the tenant

freehold
absolute ownership of real property, which will continue with no limitation of time (as against leasehold)

frustration
a contractual doctrine which relieves the parties from their liabilities under a contract if its performance becomes impossible due to the fault of neither party; frustration may apply to leases (for example, it is possible in some circumstances that a lease may be frustrated by fire)

grant
formal giving or transferring

ground rent
small sum payable periodically to the landlord (the ground owner) by tenant who holds leasehold property on a long lease

high court
the principal court which deals with civil cases in England and Wales; there is no restriction as to the amount at stake

incumbrance
any adverse interest, usually financial such as a mortgage or an undischarged debt, or a restrictive covenant limiting the use to which land may be put

joint tenants
two (or more) people who hold property jointly in such a way that when one dies the whole property automatically passes to the survivor; under the 1980 Housing Act, two or more people entitled to the right to buy

landlord
the owner of property who grants a lease or sub-lease of the property

land registry
a government department where details of properties with a registered title are recorded

lease
written contract of letting; if for more than 3 years, it must be by deed to be legal

leasehold
ownership of property for a number of years, fixed or periodic, with a lease which sets out the rights and duties of the leaseholder and the landlord (as against freehold)

legal charge
mortgage

licence
the right to use premises, as a personal privilege, without acquiring an interest in the property

offence
a breach of the criminal law

periodic tenancy
a tenancy for a short but definite period (for example, one month) which continues for such further periods until ended by notice

possession action
exercising the powers or controls of ownership; procedure whereby a landlord goes to the court to evict a tenant or other lawful residential occupier

real property
land and any buildings on it

re-entry
retaking possession of a property

registered land
when the title or ownership of freehold or leasehold property has been registered at the Land Registry and its ownership is guaranteed by the state

relief
redress, remedial action, sanctioned by law; for example where the tenant's lease is allowed by the court to continue despite the fact that the landlord has obtained a judgment for forfeiture

residential occupier
someone who lives in the property as his home

reversion
an interest in property which will eventually return to the original owner (or his successors) when the time during which another person holds the property comes to an end

secure tenant
an individual who occupies as his only or principal home a property of which the landlord is a local authority, or a county council, or a housing association or one of a few other public sector landlords

security of tenure
the right to remain in possession

service tenancy
an agreement under which an employee occupies residential accommodation for the better performance of his job

sitting tenant
popular expression for statutory tenant whose lease has expired but who is allowed by law to go on occupying the premises

statute
an act of parliament

statute law
body of law enacted in acts of parliament and their subordinate legislation (as against common law)

statutory instrument
document which makes or confirms legislation that is subordinate to
an act of parliament, such as rules, regulations, orders

sub-lease
a lease carved out of another lease, necessarily for a shorter period,
created by a person who has only a leasehold interest in the property

sub-tenant
tenant who leases property from a landlord who owns a leasehold,
not a freehold interest in that property. It is possible for a chain of
tenancies to be built up running from the freeholder (the
head-landlord) to his tenant and down to a sub-tenant, then to a
sub-sub-tenant and so on. Each tenant becomes the landlord of his
own sub-tenant down to the last link in the chain – the tenant in
actual occupation

superior landlord
someone with a higher interest than the tenant's immediate landlord;
if Mr A, a freeholder, grants a 99 year lease to Mrs B, and Mrs B
then grants a 21 year lease to Mr C, Mr A is the superior landlord

tenant
the person to whom a lease is granted

title deeds
documents going back over 15 years or longer which prove the
ownership of unregistered property

unregistered land
property – freehold or leasehold – the title or ownership of which
has not been registered at the Land Registry, so that the buyer must
investigate the validity of the seller's title to it.

Information and help

Anyone in difficulties over renting or letting, or housing rights generally, can go for advice to a **citizens advice bureau**. CAB offices have leaflets and information about local sources of help and services. The address of a local citizens advice bureau can be found in the telephone directory.

SHAC
London Housing Aid Centre
189a Old Brompton Road
London SW5 0AR   (telephone: 01-373 7841 and 01-373 7276)

gives advice and information to tenants in London who have a housing problem; can advise on what to do if you are homeless, living in bad conditions, threatened with eviction or looking for accommodation. Publications include:

Private tenants: protection from eviction   60p
Homeless? Know your rights   40p
Rights to repairs, a guide for council tenants   70p

Organisation of Private Tenants
19 Highbury Place
London N5 1QT   (telephone: 01-359 8224)

helps private tenants to form tenants' associations, publishes a regular newsletter for private tenants, hold regular meetings, advises private tenants in their relations with their landlords, increases private tenant representation at local and national level, campaigns for private tenants' rights (membership £1).

Housing Aid Trust
157 Waterloo Road
London SE1 8XF   (telephone: 01-633 9377)

has a network of eight regional housing aid centres which provide help and assistance to people with housing problems.

Shelter
National Campaign for the Homeless
157 Waterloo Road
London SE1 8XF   (telephone: 01-633 9377)

is a national organisation, with a network of groups and members, campaigning on behalf of the homeless and badly housed.

Law Centres Federation
Duchess House
18/19 Warren Street
London W1P 5DB   (telephone: 01-387 8570)
can give you details of your nearest law centre if you need legal advice.

The Department of the Environment and the Welsh Office publish a series
of (free) housing booklets, available from rent officers, council offices,
citizens advice bureaux and housing aid centres. They include:

Assured Tenancies
  A guide for landlords and tenants

Leasehold Reform
  A guide for leaseholders and landlords

Letting Rooms in your Home
  A guide for resident landlords and their tenants

Letting your Home or Retirement Home
  A guide for home-owners and servicemen who want to let their homes
  temporarily

Notice to Quit
  A brief guide for landlords and tenants

Regulated Tenancies
  Fair rents and security of tenure explained

Service Charges in Flats
  A guide for landlords and tenants

Shared Ownership
  How to become a home-owner in stages

Shorthold Tenancies
  A guide for private landlords and tenants

The Rent Acts and You
  A brief guide for landlords and tenants

Your right to buy your home
  A guide for council, new town and housing association tenants

index

consumer publications

Householder's action guide
is for everyone who owns or rents a home. It deals with problems and
decisions a householder may have to face, and what action he should take
to assert his rights and fulfil his obligations.

Topics include obtaining planning permission (and also how to stop others
getting it where their proposal would interfere with your property); the
rights and duties of local authority departments towards the householder;
rates, and how to appeal against an assessment; legal liability towards
visitors, trespassers and casual passers-by; how to deal with nuisance caused
by other people; how to avoid disputes with neighbours and, if it is
unavoidable, what action to take.

Dealing with household emergencies
aims to help the ordinary, non-too-practical person deal with urgent,
relatively straightforward jobs. It offers commonsense advice on how to
keep emergencies to a minimum, and gives detailed instructions on how to
deal with simple problems.

The contents include: knowing where to turn, electrical emergencies, how
to deal with leaks and blockages, fire-preventing and coping, window
repairs, quick action for stains, accident first aid, claiming on insurance.

Which? way to buy, sell and move house
takes the strain out of a complicated process by anticipating and answering
your questions with detailed advice. Every subject covered is tackled
logically and precisely.

Areas covered include: buying first or selling first? getting a mortgage, the
cost of moving, looking for a house, making an offer, conveyancing, buying
at an auction, selling your house, planning the move, buying and selling in
Scotland.

The legal side of buying a house
covers the procedure for buying an owner-occupied house with a registered
title in England or Wales (not Scotland). It takes you step by step through
a typical house purchase so that, in many cases, you can do your own
conveyancing, without a solicitor. It also deals with the legal side of selling.

Wills and probate

Making your own will – what to say and how to say it so that your wishes can be carried out without problems or complications, how to take advantage of capital transfer tax exemptions, and the step-by-step procedure for dealing with the administration of someone else's estate, these are the subjects of this practical layman's guide.

What will my pension be?

sets out in its three main sections what you can expect to get from the state pension, your employer's pension scheme or (if you are self employed) retirement annuities. Throughout, the tax implications are clarified, and hints given on how to improve your future pension.

Few people in their twenties and thirties anticipate what their pension will be, but when they are over fifty may wish they had planned better. By the time you reach pensionable age, it may be too late to make informed decisions: this book should therefore be read now.

Other publications include:
Approaching retirement
Avoiding back trouble
Avoiding heart trouble
Divorce – legal procedures and financial facts
Earning money at home
Getting a new job
Living with stress
Making the most of your freezer
Pregnancy month by month
Securing your home
Starting your own business
The newborn baby
The Which? book of insurance
What to do when someone dies

CA publications are available from Consumers' Association, Castlemead, Gascoyne Way, Hertford SG14 1LH, and from booksellers.